UNDI͟ THE ͟ ͟R OTHER BRONTË

by Sarah Gordon

SAMUEL FRENCH

ISBN 978-0-573-00052-2

concordtheatricals.co.uk

concordtheatricals.com

FOR AMATEUR PRODUCTION ENQUIRIES

UNITED KINGDOM AND WORLD
EXCLUDING NORTH AMERICA
licensing@concordtheatricals.co.uk

020-7054-7298

Each title is subject to availability from Concord Theatricals,
depending upon country of performance.

This work is published by Samuel French, an imprint of Concord
Theatricals Ltd.

The Professional Rights in this play are controlled by Independent
Talent Group Ltd, 40 Whitfield St, London W1T 2RH.

USE OF COPYRIGHTED MUSIC

A licence issued by Concord Theatricals to perform this play does not include permission to use the incidental music specified in this publication. In the United Kingdom: Where the place of performance is already licensed by the PERFORMING RIGHT SOCIETY (PRS) a return of the music used must be made to them. If the place of performance is not so licensed then application should be made to PRS for Music (www.prsformusic.com). A separate and additional licence from PHONOGRAPHIC PERFORMANCE LTD (www.ppluk.com) may be needed whenever commercial recordings are used. Outside the United Kingdom: Please contact the appropriate music licensing authority in your territory for the rights to any incidental music.

USE OF COPYRIGHTED THIRD-PARTY MATERIALS

Licensees are solely responsible for obtaining formal written permission from copyright owners to use copyrighted third-party materials (e.g., artworks, logos) in the performance of this play and are strongly cautioned to do so. If no such permission is obtained by the licensee, then the licensee must use only original materials that the licensee owns and controls. Licensees are solely responsible and liable for clearances of all third-party copyrighted materials, and shall indemnify the copyright owners of the play(s) and their licensing agent, Concord Theatricals Ltd., against any costs, expenses, losses and liabilities arising from the use of such copyrighted third-party materials by licensees.

IMPORTANT BILLING AND CREDIT REQUIREMENTS

If you have obtained performance rights to this title, please refer to your licensing agreement for important billing and credit requirements.

The script may have changed during rehearsals and differ from the final production

UNDERDOG: THE OTHER OTHER BRONTË was first produced at the Dorfman Theatre, National Theatre, London, a co-production with Northern Stage, Newcastle-upon-Tyne and opened on 4th April 2024. Running in Stage 1 at Northern Stage 7th–22nd June 2024. The cast was as follows:

MRS INGHAM/ELIZABETH GASKELL/ENSEMBLE .... Nick Blakeley

ANNE BRONTË .... Rhiannon Clements

MR BROCKLEHURST/THOMAS NEWBY/ENSEMBLE ....
.... Adam Donaldson

EMILY BRONTË .... Adele James

CUNLIFFE/TABBY/ENSEMBLE .... Kwaku Mills

PROFESSOR HEGER/GEORGE SMITH/ENSEMBLE ....
.... Julian Moore-Cook

BRANWELL BRONTË .... James Phoon

CHARLOTTE BRONTË .... Gemma Whelan

The production team was as follows:

DIRECTOR .... Natalie Ibu

SET AND COSTUME DESIGNER .... Grace Smart

LIGHTING DESIGNER .... Zoe Spurr

SOUND DESIGNER .... Alexandra Faye Braithwaite

MOVEMENT DIRECTOR .... Ingrid Mackinnon

FIGHT AND INTIMACY DIRECTOR .... Haruka Kuroda

CASTING .... Naomi Downham

DIALECT COACH .... Charmian Hoare

COMPANY VOICE WORK .... Shereen Ibrahim

ASSOCIATE LIGHTING DESIGNER .... Charlotte Burton

ASSOCIATE MOVEMENT DIRECTOR .... Ana Beatriz Meireles

STAFF DIRECTOR .... Natasha Haws

PRODUCER .... Fran Miller

PRODUCTION MANAGER .... Clíona Ní Mhocháin

DRAMATURG .... Stewart Pringle

COMPANY STAGE MANAGER .... Ruth Taylor

DEPUTY STAGE MANAGER .... Morag Lavery

ASSISTANT STAGE MANAGERS .... Zoe Gledhill and Ian Connop

DEPUTY PRODUCTION MANAGER .... Tabitha Piggott

PROJECT DRAUGHTING .... Tom Atkinson

DIGITAL ART .... Daniel Radley-Bennett

COSTUME SUPERVISOR . . . . Tash Prynne

ASSISTANT COSTUMER SUPERVISOR . . . . .Mariama Bojang

WIGS, HAIR & MAKE-UP SUPERVISOR . . . . .Suzanne Scotcher

RUNNING WARDROBE SUPERVISOR . . . . .Michelle MacMillan

PROPS SUPERVISOR . . . . Matilde Marangoni

PROPS BUYER . . . . Kinga Czynciel

PROPS MAKING MANAGER . . . . Michael Garrett

PROPS MAKING COORDINATOR . . . . Michelle McLucas

LIGHTING SUPERVISOR . . . . .Katie Lands

LIGHTING PROGRAMMER . . . . Reese Graham

PRODUCTION SOUND ENGINEER . . . . .Matt Berry

SOUND OPERATOR . . . . .Jacob Dicker

RADIO MICS TECHNICIAN . . . . Ethan Traynor

STAGE SUPERVISORS . . . . .Lee Harrington and Yuri Queiroz

RIGGING SUPERVISOR . . . . .James 'Luka' Goodsall

AUTOMATION . . . . .Mark Stiven and Patricia Andreucci

CONSTRUCTION SUPERVISOR . . . . .David Cotton

SCENIC ART SUPERVISOR . . . . Lindsay Tuffnell

PRODUCTION PHOTOGRAPHER . . . . .Isha Shah

The **NATIONAL THEATRE** makes theatre that entertains and inspires using its creativity, expertise and unique reach. The National Theatre shares unforgettable stories with millions of audience members across the UK and around the world – on its own stages, on tour, in schools, on cinema screens and streaming at home. World-leading artists make their best work at the National Theatre with the widest possible audience and impact. The National Theatre invests in talent and innovation on stage and off, taking seriously its role as the nation's theatre. Of the new productions developed each year with a wide range of theatre companies, a third of that research and development resource is dedicated to shows staged at theatres outside London. Through touring our work to local theatres and schools and nationwide education and community programmes, we are active in 71 of the 109 levelling up priority areas in the UK. A registered charity with deeply embedded social purpose, the National Theatre works with hundreds of schools and communities across the UK to fire imagination and inspire creativity, and to develop skills and pathways for careers in theatre. For more information, please visit nationaltheatre.org.uk

Registered Charity No: 224223
Registered as a company limited by guarantee in England: 749504

NORTHERN STAGE is a theatre that has been a part of Newcastle's cultural life since the 1970s. We make and present the very best theatre for people of the North East and beyond. Proudly Northern, our theatre is a place for people to come together to socialise, have fun, to work, think, debate, perform and to imagine new possibilities for the future. We're an Arts Council England National Portfolio Organisation, which means funding thanks to National Lottery players plays a huge part in supporting our work. For more information, please visit www.northernstage.co.uk

CHARACTERS

CHARLOTTE BRONTË
ANNE BRONTË
EMILY BRONTË

An Ensemble plays the following:

MRS INGHAM, CUNLIFFEE, SMITH, GEORGE SMITH, THOMAS NEWBY, HARRIET MARTINEAU, ELIZABETH GASKELL, TABBY, HEGER, BROCKLEHURST, BRANWELL, WESTMINSTER REVIEW, THOMAS REID, ELIZABETH RIGBY, NORTH AMERICAN REVIEW, THE SPECTATOR, THE ATLAS, QUARTERLY, CHRISTIAN REMEMBRANCER, LONDON MAGAZINE, CRITIC 2, GEORGE HENRY LEWES, FONBLANQUE, WEEKLY NEWS, LITERARY WORLD, THE ANTHENAEUM, THE ANTHENAEUM, THACKERY, THE ERA, MAY SINCLAIR, DRIVER

AUTHOR'S NOTES

Note on the text

Multiple parts played per actor. Roles should not be assigned based on gender.

The play is told from Charlotte's present day point of view and as such has a modern sensibility to it. This is reflected in dialogue. All stage direction, music and set design are suggestions only.

/   means that the next speech begins at that point.
–   means the next line interrupts.
(,) on its own means a pause equivalent to a beat.
[ ] means intended but not spoken aloud.

For Emma Gordon

PROLOGUE

(John Tavener's funereal "The Lamb" plays as the audience enter.)

(As it bleeds directly into Duran Duran's "Hungry Like The Wolf" the stage comes to life. The Ensemble erect the set, pulling up a dome of hanging male jackets of the period.)

(In the middle is **CHARLOTTE BRONTË***, directing them and checking all looks to her taste.)*

(Once done and the music has faded, the Ensemble retreat to the edges of the arena, leaving **CHARLOTTE** *at the centre.)*

CHARLOTTE. This… is not about me.

(She beams 'humbly', taking in her audience.)

Really.

EMILY. *(Offstage.)* CHARLOTTE?!

CHARLOTTE. Well, it's a little bit about me.

(Her smile fades.)

I see you all… Judging.

Young women always judge older women more harshly than anybody else in the world. Don't get me wrong, they *shout* their judgements about young men, old men… But they reserve the full weight of their arsenal for their own sex. Their mothers. Grandmothers.

Dare I say their 'idols' present and...past. They are conditioned to.

I'm aware our story's been done before. Three sisters of equal talent who supported each others' rise to fame and glory from out of the wilds of Yorkshire.

Like the centuries of women before us, we had to fight to be heard. It was a competition.

And in every competition there are winners and there are losers. And I might not be on a bank note right now *(Which is fine.)*, but, *Reader*... I think you know who's the most quotable.

You see, they say that behind every great man is a great woman.

That's nice.

But behind every great *woman* are a hundred other great women who are also trying to get her one seat at the table.

Which, let's face it, *is* awkward.

EMILY. *(Offstage.)* CHARLOTTE BRONTË –

> (**CHARLOTTE** *flinches at the interruption.*)

CHARLOTTE. Sorry –

EMILY. *(Offstage.)* WHERE THE FUCK ARE YOU?

> (*She's derailed somewhat, almost imploring.*)

CHARLOTTE. Sorry.

There may be some mistakes in this little revision.

But I – I feel you all advancing away from me again and so I fear it's time I tried to tell the truth... About how one became an idol and the other became known as the third sister.

I just... I hope you won't all judge me too harshly.

(She smiles, wryly.)

Woe betide the woman who wishes to be looked up to.

Scene One

"He's A Bellend"

*(**EMILY BRONTË** appears, holding a letter.)*

EMILY. Charlotte! There you are.

> *(As **EMILY** enters, we are transported to 1837, the Brontë household in Haworth. Above them, indistinct voices argue in the background, both male and female.)*

CHARLOTTE. *(To audience, introducing.)* Emily. Middle sister.

And above us, our brother Branwell and our father fighting, with Anne, the youngest, being very, very, very good, as ever, playing mediator.

> *(**EMILY** hands **CHARLOTTE** an envelope.)*

EMILY. Southey has replied.

CHARLOTTE. Robert Southey?!

EMILY. The very same.

> *(**CHARLOTTE** tears open the envelope.)*
>
> *(She paces about the room reading, whilst an agitated **EMILY** waits, tense.)*

CHARLOTTE. *(Hurt.)* Ha!

EMILY. Go on then, what's he said?

> *(**CHARLOTTE** freezes defensively.)*

CHARLOTTE. Nothing.

EMILY. Charlotte.

CHARLOTTE. I don't want to.

EMILY. You're not going to be a child about this are you?

CHARLOTTE. I am not being a child, I just don't want to tell you. It's my letter, it is not your letter, it's mine.

EMILY. Bloody hell.

(**ANNE BRONTË** *enters.*)

ANNE. *(Re the voices.)* They're still at it.

CHARLOTTE. *(Snapping.)* Well they can keep their problems and opinions upstairs.

Away from me.

ANNE. What – what's going on?

EMILY. Charlotte's had a reply from Robert Southey about her desire to become a professional writer.

ANNE. Baahh! Exciting! What's he said?

CHARLOTTE. "Literature cannot be the business of a woman's life, and it ought not to be" –

ANNE. Oh.

CHARLOTTE. "The more she is engaged in her proper duties, the less leisure she will have for it, even as an accomplishment and a recreation" –

EMILY. He's a bellend.

CHARLOTTE. He is the Poet Laureate!

EMILY. He's still a bellend.

CHARLOTTE. "To those duties you have not yet been called…"

EMILY. *(Grimacing.)* You told him you were single?

CHARLOTTE. "and when you are you will be less eager for celebrity" –

EMILY. You told him that you wanted to be famous?!

CHARLOTTE. I told him of my ambition to be forever known, yes.

EMILY. Oh.

CHARLOTTE. What?

EMILY. Bit much.

CHARLOTTE. What would you have had me say? "I desire your advice to become a writer of modest to little success? No, no, no, no *I* daren't ask for *anything* more than to have my talents dissolve politely into obscurity". Please. I'm not *Anne* –

ANNE. What have *I* done?!

CHARLOTTE. Nothing. You do nothing, you just stand there and listen. You look like some little church mouse.

ANNE. I do not look like a mouse. Do I look like a mouse?

EMILY. No.

CHARLOTTE. Emily –

EMILY. A bit.

> (**CHARLOTTE** *looks upwards towards the ceiling, where the voices rise again briefly in argument.*)

CHARLOTTE. *Would* they stop yelling!

EMILY. *(To* **ANNE**.*)* How are they?

ANNE. Not good.

EMILY. Branwell?

ANNE. Drunk.

EMILY. And Father?

ANNE. Weepy.

EMILY. Aunt Elizabeth?

ANNE. Irritating.

CHARLOTTE. Mighty words from the mouse!

EMILY. Stop it Charlotte.

ANNE. Father is worrying over Branwell's debts. New debts.

CHARLOTTE. Well what was he thinking? Letting him run off to try and become a painter. The man manages to turn even the most simple portrait into a nightmare in watercolours.

EMILY. At some point, Charlotte, you shall have to make peace with your nose.

CHARLOTTE. It doesn't *look* like that.

ANNE. I – I – I think he's quite good. When he's sober.

CHARLOTTE. Oh of course you do. You do nothing but serve his ego. *(Gesturing to the letter still in her hand.)* I bet you agree with this tripe. Quiet, dependant –

ANNE. Stop –

CHARLOTTE. Angelic –

ANNE. Stop it –

CHARLOTTE. Little Anne.

ANNE. Unjust!

EMILY. Please Charlotte. Leave Anne alone and go take out your rage on our dolt of a brother. Bully him into action before he drinks us out of house and home.

CHARLOTTE. Oh far be it from me to meddle in masculine matters.

> *(**EMILY** stares her down.)*

Fine.

> *(**CHARLOTTE** turns to leave. As she does so:)*

ANNE. Wait! One – one – one second.

    (**CHARLOTTE** *turns.*)

(Quietly.) I've um. I've had an idea! Actually.

CHARLOTTE. *(Rolling her eyes.)* Go on...

ANNE. If, well, if we cannot reason with our brother, as apparently we can't, then perhaps the only way out this mess is by finding our own financial independence...?

    (Both sisters look back at her blankly.)

EMILY. What?

ANNE. Like, get jobs.

CHARLOTTE. I'm not going to teach in a school again. The education system in this country is fucked.

EMILY. *(Agreeing.)* Cannot get worse.

ANNE. I agree. But – but – but what I mean to say is that whilst teaching is really the only thing we might be qualified for that is respectable and, and, um –

CHARLOTTE. Oh *please* get to the point –

ANNE. I have applied for a role as a governess.

CHARLOTTE. What?

ANNE. At a manor house. In Mirfield.

CHARLOTTE. You? Governess?

ANNE. Yes! What do you think?

CHARLOTTE. You?

ANNE. Yes, me!

    (**ANNE** *waits a moment in suspense as* **CHARLOTTE** *considers this.*)

CHARLOTTE. No.

ANNE. I thought, if I were to attain such a position, then I would, well, A) be able to acquire something of my own independence –

CHARLOTTE. *(To* **EMILY***, playfully.)* She's doing that listing thing –

ANNE. – And B)! Be able to send some of my salary back home.

EMILY. And you have already acquired the position?

ANNE. I have!

EMILY. *(To* **CHARLOTTE***.)* Hardly mouse behaviour!

ANNE. I – I really am not a mouse! I – I only wish to do what is best.

*(***ANNE*** and ***EMILY*** both look to ***CHARLOTTE***.)*

CHARLOTTE. No.

EMILY. What?!

CHARLOTTE. She will not be able to bear it.

EMILY. And why do you think that?

CHARLOTTE. Because I know, as well as you do, that governessing is vile, lonely, debasing work, teaching table manners to aristocratic brats with egos larger than Queen Victoria's arse. Anne would not last a week.

EMILY. Anne is stronger than you think.

CHARLOTTE. Anne is a mouse!

ANNE. *(Mumbled.)* Anne is in the room.

CHARLOTTE. Beg your pardon?

ANNE. N – nothing.

CHARLOTTE. *(To* **EMILY***.)* You see how meek she is! She's is too gentle for that sort of work.

EMILY. Hypocrite! You sound like the pompous twat who wrote that letter!

CHARLOTTE. I most certainly do not!

EMILY. You would stop Anne from pursuing her dream –

ANNE. Oh, it's really not my dream –

EMILY. Stay out of this Anne –

ANNE. Sorry.

CHARLOTTE. I am protecting her. School nearly killed her!

ANNE. But this isn't school, it's a manor house. A big manor house. With things like food.

EMILY. *(To* **CHARLOTTE**.*)* The circumstances are entirely different.

CHARLOTTE. We will think of something else.

EMILY. We need the money now.

ANNE. Please.

> *(Small pause.)*

CHARLOTTE. It's for your own good that I am saying no.

EMILY. Christ! You know we're all screwed financially, don't you?

> *(***CHARLOTTE*** *retreats to a chair to brood over her letter.)*

CHARLOTTE. I will think of something.

EMILY. *(To* **ANNE**.*)* She can't stop you, you know.

CHARLOTTE. *(To audience.)* Not true.

ANNE. No, I … Maybe I can find employment at home.

EMILY. Urgh. You're an idiot. *(To* **CHARLOTTE**.*) You're* a dick. I'm going to sort out Branwell.

> *(***EMILY*** *exits.)*

*(**ANNE** hovers, watching **CHARLOTTE** read.)*

(She sits and picks up a book. Pretends to read.)

(Small pause.)

CHARLOTTE. I can feel you watching me.

ANNE. Sorry.

Sorry.

> *(**ANNE** picks up her book again. Pretends to read. Watches **CHARLOTTE**.)*

(Small pause.)

CHARLOTTE. *(Not looking up.)* What is it?

ANNE. I – I'm really sorry about Southey.

CHARLOTTE. Don't be.

ANNE. *I* believe in you. Your stories are *amazing* –

CHARLOTTE. Thanks Anne, I'm just. I'm not in the mood.

ANNE. Sorry.

Sorry.

> *(Small pause. **ANNE** grins.)*

Hey, um. Do – do your 'man' impression.

CHARLOTTE. Not now Anne.

ANNE. Go on.

CHARLOTTE. Stop it, I said I'm not in the mood.

ANNE. *(Already giggling.)* Do – do the bit where you're like Lord Byron.

CHARLOTTE. Anne –

ANNE. *Please* –

CHARLOTTE. *(As Lord Byron.)* FUCK OFF YOU PAGAN SHIT OF A WOMAN!

(**ANNE** *screams with excitement.*)

ANNE. OH MY GOD IT'S SO GOOD!!

(**CHARLOTTE** *rises.*)

CHARLOTTE. *(Still as Lord Byron.)* Draw your pistol or be damned!!

(*Delighted,* **ANNE** *draws out a mime pistol. The pair of them mime shoot each other,* **CHARLOTTE** *still as Lord Byron – everything groin first.*)

Now kiss me you bitch!

(**ANNE** *dies with giggles, struggling to breath.*)

ANNE. I can't – I can't – I can't –

(**CHARLOTTE** *laughs with her.*)

CHARLOTTE. Alright, calm down.

ANNE. I can't – I can't...

(*After their laughter has died out,* **CHARLOTTE** *slumps back into her chair.* **ANNE** *sits by* **CHARLOTTE**'s *feet. She puts her head on her lap.*)

Play with my hair.

CHARLOTTE. No.

ANNE. Pleeeeaaase.

(**CHARLOTTE** *huffs, but strokes* **ANNE**'s *hair.*)

(*Small pause.*)

CHARLOTTE. *(Morose.)* I would be an *excellent* Lord.

ANNE. You would.

CHARLOTTE. Mm.

ANNE. It's going to be alright. Emily's right. Southey's a – a you know. A *(Quietly.)* … Bellend.

CHARLOTTE. Wow.

ANNE. Sorry –

CHARLOTTE. Convincing.

ANNE. Well, I don't get why you have to ask for his permission? You write anyway.

CHARLOTTE. Oh Anne.

ANNE. I'm serious!

CHARLOTTE. Because!

Because.

Listen, men – writers – like him are the gatekeepers. Whoever is in that room with them has the power to dictate what is acceptable and what is not, and I *need* what I think be be acceptable.

I spend more hours trying to deny myself the thoughts I have because I know as a woman I shouldn't have them than the hours I spend writing them down anyway. It's fucked.

ANNE. I agree. I get it.

CHARLOTTE. To be someone like him, to be someone like Southey or Byron, your thoughts are untouchable. You can think what you like and you can say what you like… *That's* why I told him I want to be 'forever known'. I want to be as free and as bullet proof as they are.

(**ANNE** *nods.*)

ANNE. Then you will be. You'll get there.

(**CHARLOTTE** *smiles.*)

CHARLOTTE. God I can only say this shit to you. *(Re* **EMILY**.*)* She wouldn't get it.

ANNE. Oh she would.

(**CHARLOTTE** *raises her eyebrows.*)

She just doesn't get 'rules'.

(**CHARLOTTE** *laughs a little.*)

CHARLOTTE. I'm sorry about the governessing thing. It's just – it's *really* shitty work.

ANNE. Yeah… I guess I just want to be useful.

CHARLOTTE. But you're so delicate!

ANNE. I'm really not, I just *look* delicate.

CHARLOTTE. *(Light.)* Oh piss off Anne.

ANNE. We want the same things though. We both want change, we both want freedom.

CHARLOTTE. Being a governess is not / being free.

(/ *They're interrupted as* **BRANWELL** *crashes into the room, flamboyantly livid, with a completely soaked shirt, face and wet hair.* **CHARLOTTE** *and* **ANNE** *snort with laughter.*)

What happened to you?

BRANWELL. *Emily happened.*

(*He shakes some of the water off himself. His manner is effeminate and highly strung.*)

You know, for someone who thinks she's good with words she doesn't use them very much.

CHARLOTTE. Well, what were you arguing about?

BRANWELL. Doesn't matter!

CHARLOTTE. Branwell...

BRANWELL. Nothing! You wouldn't understand! You have NO IDEA the kind of pressure I'm under.

> *(**ANNE** and **CHARLOTTE** exchange a look.)*

> *(**BRANWELL** melodramatically falls at **CHARLOTTE**'s feet and plonks his head in her lap, sitting beside **ANNE**.)*

Play with my hair.

> *(Entertained in spite of herself, **CHARLOTTE** rolls her eyes and affectionately strokes his hair – we see that he's always kind of been one of the girls... Until this recent issue.)*

CHARLOTTE. What pressure?

BRANWELL. To be the breadwinner! The one supporting all of you. Doesn't matter if it goes directly at odds with what *I* want to do. I mean, can you honest to God see me in a dog collar? I don't think so hun.

*(To **ANNE**.)* Pass me that brandy.

> *(**ANNE** does so, reluctantly.)*

CHARLOTTE. What did dad say?

> *(**BRANWELL** pours and drinks, head still in her lap.)*

BRANWELL. He thinks it's time for a change in direction. That the art studio isn't working out.

> *(**CHARLOTTE** glances at **ANNE** over **BRANWELL**'s head.)*

CHARLOTTE. Oh, noo...

BRANWELL. Right?! I mean, *you* like my work, don't you?

CHARLOTTE. *(Forced light.)* Yes!

It's great!

Really great.

I think you're really great at painting.

No-one... Paints better than you.

> *(**ANNE** rolls her eyes.)*

BRANWELL. I mean, can't you just see me in the National Portrait Gallery?

CHARLOTTE. *(To audience.)* The irony.

*(To **BRANWELL**.)* Um, maybe!

ANNE. *(Also forced.)* Yeah, maybe!

> *(Sensing his sisters tone, **BRANWELL** sits up and spins round angrily to face them. We see how quickly his moods can turn, from pouty and hammy to volatile and aggressive.)*

BRANWELL. What? Why do you look like that?

CHARLOTTE. Look like what?

BRANWELL. Like you have a raw onion in your mouth.

CHARLOTTE. That's just my face –

BRANWELL. No, you're looking like you doubt me! Like you hate my painting!

CHARLOTTE. I don't *hate* your painting... I just –

> *(**BRANWELL** springs up, livid.)*

BRANWELL. Oh my GOD!!

CHARLOTTE. I just don't know if painting is your greatest strength –

(**BRANWELL** *suddenly hurls his brandy glass at the wall – it smashes.*)

(*Shocked,* **CHARLOTTE** *and* **ANNE** *flinch, cower and then back off in practised wariness. Speech is muddied:*)

BRANWELL. Do you have any idea what it's like?! –

ANNE. (*Gently, imploring.*) Branwell!!

CHARLOTTE. What the (?!) –

BRANWELL. – To be constantly undermined by you lot?!

> (*He paces about, talking in a way that is both melodramatic and felt, performative and real in its violence all at once.*)

(*Furious, rushed.*) Everyone pulling punches – these incessant opinions – everyone thinking they're all so above me, whilst also looking to me – to *me* – to be the one to bring home the bloody bacon until someone marries you and takes you off my hands! Which, by the way, means bringing home the bloody bacon until the END OF DAYS because who on God's green earth is going to want to marry any of you / lot

> (/ **EMILY** *enters and throws another bucket of water at* **BRANWELL**'s *head. It stops him in his tracks.*)

> (**ANNE** *lets out a shocked and nervous giggle.*)

> (**BRANWELL** *spins round to face* **EMILY**, *spitting out a bit of water.*)

WOULD YOU *PLEASE* STOP DOING THAT?!

EMILY. (*Unfazed.*) I think we've heard enough.

BRANWELL. (*Yelling.*) Daddy! She's throwing water at me again! Daddy!

EMILY. *(Re their dad.)* Be quiet, he's praying.

BRANWELL. Yes, but hc'll be praying *for* me, so effectively I'm just answering him.

CHARLOTTE. But, to be fair, I don't think that's the response he'll be wanting.

> (**CHARLOTTE** *smiles trying to lighten the mood, but* **BRANWELL** *sighs, suddenly deflated and morose at this last.)*

> *(A small pause.)*

BRANWELL. No.

No, I never say what he wants.

I'm not what any of them want.

(Re their dad / other men.) I'm not like them.

Am I?

> (**CHARLOTTE** *looks back at him with genuine sympathy.)*

CHARLOTTE. Branwell, it's going to be –

> *(He bats her off with a hand.)*

BRANWELL. Don't.

> *(He exits, taking the brandy bottle with him.)*

> *(The sisters stand in silence together for a moment.)*

CHARLOTTE. *(To **ANNE**.)* Go to Mirfield. Take the position.

> (**EMILY** *nods, agreeing.)*

ANNE. You mean it?

CHARLOTTE. You're right. We need change. We need to earn. Now.

Scene Two

"Cunliffe"

(Lofty classical music plays as **ANNE** *looks up at imposing face and doors of Blake Hall, holding onto the back of her bonnet as she looks upwards so it doesn't fall off.)*

ANNE. *(Whispered to herself.)* Bloody hell.

(The doors open in to a tower of light.)

MRS INGHAM. Anne Brontë?

ANNE. *(Nervously.)* Yes… It is I.

*(***ANNE*** grimaces. That came out weird.)*

(She steps into the house.)

MRS INGHAM. Mrs Ingham.

ANNE. Anne Brontë.

MRS INGHAM. As we have already established.

ANNE. Oh yes! Hahahahahaha.

Yes.

Sorry.

I am a little nervous.

MRS INGHAM. Oh aren't you cute. They'll devour cute.

Come along.

*(***ANNE*** *follows* **MRS INGHAM** *through the corridors of the house for the grand tour.)*

I have four children; three girls, Mary, Martha and Emily; and a boy, Cunliffe.

ANNE. Cunliffe?

MRS INGHAM. Yes.

ANNE. His name is Cunliffe?

MRS INGHAM. Yes. What seems to be the problem?

ANNE. Nothing.

MRS INGHAM. Good.

Now. You shall only be teaching Martha, Emily and Cunliffe because Mary is only two and to teach her would be stupid. You will school them in all of the essentials. Latin, Mathematics, painting, reading, French and music. You will teach Cunliffe separately on some occasions as he's a boy, so naturally deserves more attention.

ANNE. Naturally.

MRS INGHAM. When teaching my children you are not permitted to reprimand them, intimidate them or threaten them in any way. That is my privilege... And you are to remember at all times that though they are not yet ten years old, they are your masters and mistresses. You are here to better their education as a service *for* them. Is that clear?

ANNE. Very clear.

MRS INGHAM. Good.

> (**MRS INGHAM** *pauses and gestures towards a vase.*)

This used to belong to the Queen.

ANNE. Gosh.

MRS INGHAM. Yes.

> (*They move on.*)

As you are not a lady you will naturally not dine with the family. But as you are trusted with teaching the etiquette of the nobility to my children you are not to dine with the servants either, to prevent you from picking up their ungodly habits. Or the smell.

Instead you will dine alone. And after you have dined alone you shall retire to your room alone. Any time you are not with my children in fact, you shall spend completely alone.

ANNE. How am I to receive my meals Ma'm? Without communicating with the servants?

MRS INGHAM. *(Dumbfounded.)* I, um... Food just tends to appear, I ...

> *(She shrugs.)*

ANNE. Very good.

MRS INGHAM. Oh, lastly. We have had several governess here before and I feel I ought to mention... My husband and I have a lovely marriage. Let's keep it that way, shall we?

ANNE. Of course.

MRS INGHAM. Good.

Cunliffe?

> *(**CUNLIFFE** runs on.)*

Meet your new governess. Miss Brontë.

> *(**CUNLIFFE** blows an enormous, long raspberry in **ANNE**'s face. **ANNE** smiles tightly.)*

ANNE. Oh he is *charming!*

> *(**CUNLIFFE** starts to yell... One constant long yell at the top of his lungs, pausing only for breath. **ANNE** and **MRS INGHAM**'s dialogue*

is yelled over the top of **CUNLIFFE***'s din – fleeting interchanges across the weeks:)*

Cunliffe!

MRS INGHAM. Miss Brontë, the noise!

/

ANNE. Cunliffe, please –

MRS INGHAM. Miss Brontë!

/

You may not speak to my son in this manner! He is your master!

ANNE. But, I –

/

MRS INGHAM. Miss Brontë control him!

ANNE. But how am I to control him if I cannot scold him?!

MRS INGHAM. You find a way, or you leave this house.

ANNE. *(To herself.)* I cannot go home. I will not go home…

> *(***ANNE*** moves to control* **CUNLIFFE***, but he smacks her across the face.)*

> *(Both* **ANNE** *and* **CUNLIFFE** *stand back from each other in stunned silence.* **MRS INGHAM** *also remains watching over them as* **CUNLIFFE** *pulls a little nest of baby birds from his bag and lays it on the ground. Twittering from within.)*

> *(He scoops up one of the birds.* **ANNE** *stands back, wary.)*

(Gently.) Cunliffe. Please.

(**CUNLIFFE** *does not raise his attention away from the bird.*)

CUNLIFFE. Go away.

ANNE. Think of what is kind. They are innocent young things.

CUNLIFFE. My father gave them to me. I want to pluck each of their feathers from them one by one to see how long it might take for them to die.

ANNE. I do not believe you wish to do such a thing.

(**CUNLIFFE** *plucks a feather from the bird. It screams with pain.*)

CUNLIFFE. See! See how much the stupid thing screams? And think how many feathers it has!

ANNE. Please. Stop.

CUNLIFFE. It wriggles funny in my hand.

(**CUNLIFFE** *plucks another feather. More screaming.*)

ANNE. Cunliffe you are to stop this right now.

CUNLIFFE. You cannot order me!

ANNE. I said *STOP*!

(**CUNLIFFE** *laughs at her whilst plucking another feather.*)

(*Desperate,* **ANNE** *grabs a large stone from the garden path, dashes over to the nest and slams the stone over it, crushing the birds.* **CUNLIFFE** *looks over at her shocked, then runs away.*)

*(As he does so he releases the bird he had held in his hands. **ANNE** watches it fly away, starting to hyperventilate.)*

I will not stand by – I will not –

*(Distraught, **ANNE** brings herself to look back to **MRS INGHAM**.)*

It is unjust! It is unjust and vile behaviour and I will not stand by and let it happen!

MRS INGHAM. Then you shall be dismissed.

*(**ANNE** rises, angry.)*

ANNE. You shall be exposed… You have treated me like I am barely human.

You teach your children to treat the world as such. You are unjust and you shall be exposed.

MRS INGHAM. Oh Miss Brontë, I hardly believe even this small corner of the world will ever be able to hear what *you* have to say. Such a pitiable, *little* voice you have… Such a shame you choose to try to make it shout. You could have been a perfect little lady.

*(**MRS INGHAM** disappears.)*

*(**ANNE** picks up a piece of chalk and starts to frantically write what has just happened across the floor. Words that form part of what will become* Agnes Grey.*)*

*(She's quickly distracted by **CHARLOTTE**, sending a letter her way:)*

CHARLOTTE. Dearest Anne, Can't begin to express how sorry I am that you had to go through that. Arseholes. Sending hugs.

ANNE. Dearest Charlotte, Thanks. I still can't sleep, I can't *believe* the way these people are allowed to behave! To think women up and down the country are treated like this. To bear witness and to *serve* this. Something has to be done... Hugs back.

CHARLOTTE. Dearest Anne, you coming home then?

ANNE. Dearest Charlotte, *no*, like I said, I am going to persevere and find a new position.

CHARLOTTE. Dearest Anne, Fine. I wish you loads and loads and loads of luck with finding a new awesome position teaching murderous aristocratic dickheads.

ANNE. Dearest Charlotte, If you're going to be mean, I'm not writing to you any more.

(**CHARLOTTE** *rolls her eyes.*)

Besides. I – I – I have determined to ask my new employer for more money. If I am going to work as a doormat at least I might hope to get paid properly for it.

CHARLOTTE. Well that's never going to happen. But you give it a go mousey!

(To audience.) I meanwhile...

(Back to **ANNE**.*)* Am going to Belgium!

ANNE. What?! Why?

CHARLOTTE. Because I have *tried* to deny myself, but I cannot stop writing. So I've arranged for Emily and I to go together. We'll make it look as though we're studying to set up a school, but really we're going to hone our craft. I'm going to turn this into a profession once and for all.

ANNE. Oh! Oh, that's... That's cool.

CHARLOTTE. I will not give up.

ANNE. And – and you go together?

CHARLOTTE. Yes.

ANNE. When?

CHARLOTTE. We leave Monday next.

ANNE. I see.

CHARLOTTE. What's the matter?

ANNE. Nothing, I … *(Small, embarrassed.)* Just… You didn't ask me.

CHARLOTTE. To what?

ANNE. To come with you.

CHARLOTTE. Oh. Well I thought you wanted to governess (?)

ANNE. Yes… Yeah… You're right.

CHARLOTTE. And we cannot stay here. Branwell is getting worse with every job he loses. He spends our money, threatens our own father and we are powerless to stop him. It's time we joined you and all took matters into our own hands.

ANNE. Yes… Yes. Sorry. Sorry. You two are such brilliant writers, it makes sense.

CHARLOTTE. Your support means everything. Hugs, Charlotte.

> *(**ANNE** disappears as **CHARLOTTE** turns back to the audience.)*

And so Emily and I went to Belgium. Where I met –

> *(She stops herself.)*

Where I met… Um.

> *(**MR HEGER** appears. **CHARLOTTE** sees him. She runs across the space and they embrace, passionately.)*

> (**CHARLOTTE** *addresses the audience, beaming, smug as hell; whilst he cradles her.*)

Monsieur Heger.

My professor.

I KNOW.

Oh my God, he was the most gorgeous, fiery, insanely intelligent man – who happened to be married – but who actually seemed to *respect* me and my work.

Everything I wrote was with him in mind – would he like it? What would he find the most impressive? My turn of phrase was *on fire*. And then he would critique me, he'd tear it to shreds and we would talk and talk for *hours*. He would say things like –

MR HEGER. You 'ave a peculiar mind.

CHARLOTTE. And –

MR HEGER. Zis is a Belgian Waffle.

CHARLOTTE. And I was in heaven.

Me! Plain Yorkshireish me!

In Europe! Here with this man. This man who, who...

> (**MR HEGER** *disappears over the next:*)

Who I really, really thought loved me back.

> (*Beat.*)

> (*She smiles, embarrassed.*)

Months of unanswered letters.

> (*Self-conscious, she shakes it off – back to light bravado.*)

Try having *that* in the British Library.

Clearly I was too much for him... And, as it turned out, Belgium is actually totally shit anyway, so I went back to England.

ANNE. Dearest Charlotte, haven't heard from you in ages. You OK?

>   (**CHARLOTTE** *avoids eye contact.*)

CHARLOTTE. I wasn't ignoring her, I was just, you know, embarrassed.

ANNE. Dear Charlotte, helllooooo?!

CHARLOTTE. You've see the difference between us. I know you have –

ANNE. Is it something I've done?

CHARLOTTE. I mean, *she's*... Beautiful.

ANNE. I hope we're OK –

CHARLOTTE. She could never understand rejection.

ANNE. Well, just writing anyway... Just wanted to tell you I've gotten a position at Thorpe Green at double the salary, if you please. £30 per year babaayyyy!

>   (**CHARLOTTE** *mouths a baffled "WHAT?!"*
>   *To herself and, now huffy, continues to not*
>   *respond to* **ANNE**.)

Um.

Thought you might be proud.

Anyway... Write back would you, I – I'm actually bit nervous.

CHARLOTTE. I have my mind, I told myself. At least I have my mind.

>   (*Disheartened from* **CHARLOTTE**'s *lack*
>   *of response,* **ANNE** *gathers her things and*
>   *prepares to enter Thorpe Green.*)

(**CHARLOTTE** *turns away to write across the floor her opening passages of what will become* The Professor *as* **ANNE** *knocks at the doors to Thorpe Green.*)

(*She enters, in darkness. Around her are whispering, gossipy* **VOICE***'s of the household staff. In the candlelight, they are shadowy and disorientating to* **ANNE**.*)

ANNE. Hello?

VOICE. Follow me.

Have you seen her?

She's pale.

You're to eat here.

Alone.

Too young to be a governess.

ANNE. Excuse me?

VOICE. Lessons will begin each morning from eight.

She'll have no command over them.

ANNE. Who said that?

VOICE. After lessons you will return to your rooms.

Alone.

She's plain.

ANNE. I can *hear* you, you know.

VOICE. So plain she hardly seems noticeable.

This is where you shall sleep.

(*Her anxiety turning into anger,* **ANNE** *kneels and starts to write from* Agnes Grey:)

Alone.

I do not like the look of her.

There is nothing to like. She is featureless.

Do all governesses remain alone forever?

Yes.

How do they bear it?

Why should we care?

Single forever!

They are either too high or too low, which means they belong to no-one. And they *think* they know everything, but have nothing to give, which makes them unloveable to everyone.

> (**ANNE** *slams down her piece of chalk.*)

ANNE. *ENOUGH!*

> (*The shadowy chorus of staff back off, stunned.* **ANNE** *is fleetingly proud of finding her voice and commanding respect, before:*)

CHARLOTTE. *(To audience.)* After finding our brother employment at the same household as her, Branwell thanked Anne in the only way a fuckwit can... by starting an affair with her employer.

> (*Daylight.* **MRS ROBINSON**, **ANNE***'s employer, stands beside her, presenting* **ANNE***'s suitcase to her by way of dismissal.* **ANNE** *takes it, mortified and exits the house, travelling home with* **BRANWELL** *– who looks markedly more embittered and drained.*)

Brilliant. This is what we were working with. Behaviour that wasn't *meant* to be vindictive... Just 'thoughtless'. Not only did he get himself fired, but his indiscretion cost Anne her job too.

Welcome to the Victorian age of enlightenment! Where you only need to be stood in the next room to someone having sex and somehow *you* get the sack... And you wonder why we didn't smile in photos. We were horny and terrified and fucking livid.

Scene Three

"Messers Currer, Ellis and Acton Bell"

(**CHARLOTTE** and **ANNE** writing in the same room, but separately.)

(**ANNE** pauses to look over at **CHARLOTTE**, head bent down low over her work.)

ANNE. (Tentative.) Charlotte?

CHARLOTTE. Not now.

ANNE. Sorry.

Sorry.

(**ANNE** gets back to her own writing.)

(Silence for a moment as the two continue to work, but soon **ANNE** gets distracted by glancing at her big sister again, clearly knowing she shouldn't interrupt, but unable to stop herself:)

What are you writing?

(**CHARLOTTE** flinches, irritated.)

CHARLOTTE. A book.

ANNE. A whole book?

CHARLOTTE. Yes.

ANNE. Wow.

CHARLOTTE. Sure.

ANNE. What's it about?

CHARLOTTE. (Short.) I'll tell you when it's finished.

ANNE. Of course. Sorry... Sorry.

(**CHARLOTTE** *bends back to her work.* **ANNE**
follows suit.)

(,)

Um, Charlotte?

CHARLOTTE. *(Forced, light.)* I might go write in my room.

ANNE. Oh. Sorry.

CHARLOTTE. Did you *need* something Anne?

ANNE. Oh. No. No, it's nothing.

(**CHARLOTTE** *looks at her pointedly.*)

(Shyly.) It's just, um… Well, I've been writing a novel
too.

CHARLOTTE. S'cuse me?

ANNE. I wondered if you might read it for me.

CHARLOTTE. You've already finished it?!

ANNE. Well, yes. It's based on the diaries I kept whilst
governessing.

CHARLOTTE. You – you wrote the whole time you were
governessing?

ANNE. *(Yeah.)* It's like an authentic portrayal of what it's
really like to work for the social elite. How a governess –
someone as ordinary as you or I, finds liberty from
within herself whilst trapped in her position.

CHARLOTTE. Oh… OK.

ANNE. It's a terrible idea. You hate it. (?)

CHARLOTTE. No, no…

ANNE. Because – because it's not just that. There's also a
love story. But I don't know if it's any good. So, I – I

guess I'm asking if you would, um, if you might read it for me?

CHARLOTTE. Sure… Sorry, I just didn't realise that writing was like your *thing* I guess.

ANNE. *(Bashful.)* Oh! Yeah… I know I'm not like 'the writer' – obviously!

It's no way near as good as your stories.

CHARLOTTE. Of course.

ANNE. Of course.

CHARLOTTE. But that just cos it's not your thing…

ANNE. No. No, exactly…

CHARLOTTE. What's it called? This 'book'?

ANNE. It's called 'Passages From The Life Of An Individual'.

CHARLOTTE. *(Flatly.)* Catchy.

ANNE. I would love to see what you make of it.

CHARLOTTE. Mmhm!

ANNE. And, um, Emily said you were writing about your time in Brussels with Mr –

CHARLOTTE. I don't want to talk about it.

(To audience.) It's not about me.

ANNE. OK. Sorry.

CHARLOTTE. *(Back to **ANNE**, lofty.)* It's about power and submission.

ANNE. Wow.

CHARLOTTE. I know.

ANNE. See, this is why I need you to read it. I need someone like you to tell me if it's any good or not, before I try and – and – and –

CHARLOTTE. Oh my God you're planning on taking it to a publisher?!

ANNE. Well... I thought I might do, yes.

CHARLOTTE. You're not serious.

ANNE. Um, well, yes I – I – I think I might be serious.

I don't want to be 'in the room' like you exactly. But I wrote this in order to expose the system, to instruct. And instruction needs a classroom.

CHARLOTTE. Right. Huh.

ANNE. You don't think I should?

CHARLOTTE. No... It's just... This isn't something I ever imagined *you* would want. I mean...

Writing is life, Anne. It is loud.

ANNE. I know... And I want to live.

> (**ANNE** *speaks the next in the tone of wanting to prove herself, rather than defensively:*)

Charlotte, it's not society, it's not men who have built my character... It's you. I am only small as your little sister. Nowhere else. But I am loud on the page. I promise.

CHARLOTTE. I see.

ANNE. I know it's mad, I know it's an impossible business for us... But I thought if we did it *together* then we might actually stand a chance of being heard. I mean, one person breaking the rules might look like madness, but two or three starts to look like a – like a movement.

CHARLOTTE. *(Impressed.)* OK ...

I just... I thought you liked teaching?

ANNE. I never said I liked teaching.

CHARLOTTE. *(Defensively.)* Alright – chill out.

(**CHARLOTTE** *thinks.*)

I mean, obviously I have been thinking about this for ages, because writing has always been like –

ANNE. Your thing.

CHARLOTTE. Still my thing.

But I think we might actually be onto something here.

ANNE. You mean *I* might be onto something.

CHARLOTTE. Yeah that's what I said.

But I think if we are to do this together, then I think we should start with an anthology of poetry.

ANNE. Poetry?

CHARLOTTE. Poems are quicker and easier to make it into print. We'll build ourselves a reputation, then the novels will stand a greater chance of being read.

ANNE. Yeah, OK. Just… I'm not sure I'm *that* great at poetry.

CHARLOTTE. Me neither… But Emily is.

(**ANNE** *frowns.*)

ANNE. How do you know?

(**CHARLOTTE** *turns to the audience.*)

CHARLOTTE. Because I broke into her room, riffled through her drawers, found her secret stash of poems marked *PRIVATE* and nicked them.

I'm not proud… But Emily never got the whole 'art-needing-an-audience' thing, so if I hadn't done it you would have all been denied some of the most amazing poetry in the English language. So, again, don't be judgy.

(**EMILY** *appears across the stage, incensed, holding an empty drawer.*)

I tried to convince her that –

(*To* **EMILY**.) IT'S FOR THE GOOD OF WOMEN KIND!

EMILY. GIVES A SHIT, THAT'S *MY STUFF! DON'T GO THROUGH MY STUFF –*

(**EMILY** *hurls the empty drawer at her.* **CHARLOTTE** *dodges it.*)

CHARLOTTE. (*To audience.*) But Emily was big on privacy.

(**CHARLOTTE** *picks up the drawer and takes it back to* **EMILY** *as she continues to address the audience.*)

Eventually she came round to the idea and we started to work together.

(**EMILY** *and* **ANNE** *takes their seats around a desk, planning.* **EMILY** *is technically on board, but still hasn't forgiven* **CHARLOTTE**.*)

This is how women lift each other up. *This* is how voices come to be heard. / *This* –

ANNE. (*Interrupting.*) / This desk wobbles.

(*Irritated,* **CHARLOTTE** *turns into the scene.*)

CHARLOTTE. Can we all concentrate please?

ANNE. Sorry. Concentrating.

EMILY. Concentrating *Charlotte*.

(**CHARLOTTE** *glances distractedly at* **EMILY** *repeatedly over the next:*)

CHARLOTTE. Right. My main concern is Branwell.

ANNE. Yes.

EMILY. Yes *Charlotte*.

CHARLOTTE. If he finds out that we are starting to work together, then all hell will break loose.

ANNE. Yes.

EMILY. Yes *Charlotte*.

CHARLOTTE. The question is how to avoid personal publicity, whilst making a name for ourselves.

ANNE. Yes.

EMILY. Yes *Char / lotte* –

CHARLOTTE. *(To* **EMILY**.*) Will you stop it!*

EMILY. Stop what? –

ANNE. What is it? –

CHARLOTTE. She's looking at my nose! She's not looking at me in the eyes when I speak.

EMILY. I'm looking at your face.

CHARLOTTE. You are *pointedly* looking at my nose.

EMILY. I cannot look at your face without looking at your nose. Is your nose on your face?

CHARLOTTE. You *know* what you're doing.

ANNE. Emily... –

EMILY. Is her nose on her face?

ANNE. Well, yes.

EMILY. Well, I cannot look at her face without looking at her nose.

CHARLOTTE. It's the *way* you're looking at it.

EMILY. How am I looking at it?

CHARLOTTE. Like you have a problem with it.

EMILY. I mean, it sounds like you're projecting –

CHARLOTTE. *(To **ANNE**.)* She's baiting me!

ANNE. You have a *lovely* nose. Emily stop looking at her nose.

CHARLOTTE. Look. If we are going to do this then you are going to have to forgive me.

EMILY. Oh I do, do I?

CHARLOTTE. Well, yes –

EMILY. Oh *do* I?

CHARLOTTE. Yes!

ANNE. I – I think you do –

EMILY. Why?

ANNE. Oh, well, you promised me you would. And we're all here now, so...

EMILY. ... Fine.

ANNE. *(Weakly.)* Yaaay!

(**ANNE** *turns back to* **CHARLOTTE**.)

CHARLOTTE. As I was saying... The problem, I fear, is Branwell or Papa discovering us.

EMILY. *(Dryly.)* Oh the shame of it.

CHARLOTTE. Much of what we write, women have no business in writing.

EMILY. And yet, it is written.

CHARLOTTE. Are you still being difficult?

EMILY. No, I'm just saying. You said that what we've written women aren't allowed to write, but we've already written it, so...

CHARLOTTE. If she's going to be like this then I don't want to bother.

ANNE. I think what she means, Emily, is that whilst we might have *written* it, the works still would not be *read*... Justly... Without attacking our sense of propriety, our femininity.

EMILY. So?

CHARLOTTE. So?! So, you're a woman, you know the deal. Propriety equals reputation, reputation equals money, money equals food, food equals life, no food equals death. Welcome to 1845. Jesus.

(**EMILY** *and* **CHARLOTTE** *have a brief stare off.*)

EMILY. Fine.

(*,*)

ANNE. Unless... We write as men.

(*She has her sisters' attention.*)

Pseudonyms. Male pseudonyms will protect our reputations and allow the *work* to be judged from a place of equality.

CHARLOTTE. Go on.

ANNE. If we send out our poems as three *male* authors then they still might not be published, but at least we shall be judged as equals.

(*Small pause.*)

EMILY. If it grants us anonymity then I agree.

ANNE. Really?

EMILY. Great plan.

CHARLOTTE. To walk invisible.

ANNE. Exactly!

CHARLOTTE. Just imagine… To not have to bother with ideas of perfection. Of our thoughts being 'ladylike'. It's genius. I can't believe I didn't think of it sooner.

ANNE. It was *my* idea –

CHARLOTTE. Yeah, that's what I meant.

EMILY. But we can't tell anyone.

CHARLOTTE. No. The secrecy is our liberation. It is binding. One mask worn by all three of us.

EMILY. Yes.

ANNE. What shall we call ourselves?

CHARLOTTE. Let us be The Brothers Bell, for our voices will ring out as brightly as the bells from father's church.

ANNE. Aw that's lovely.

CHARLOTTE. Sure. Just take a name that begins with the same letter as yours…

Like, I'll be…

> (*As they decide upon their names, they pull three male jackets down from above.*)

Currer Bell.

EMILY. Ellis Bell.

> (**ANNE** *puffs herself up, 'man–like'.*)

ANNE. Acton Bell!

CHARLOTTE. Perfect.

> (*They each don their jackets,* **CHARLOTTE** *wearing hers like it was made for her, her posture moulded into a more 'masculine' stance. She addresses the audience.*)

In the end, the collected works of Currer, Ellis and
Acton Bell only found a readership of, um, two people.
But we won't go into that –that's not important. The
point is, we'd started something.

Scene Four

"It's a 'No'"

(The space becomes fluid, allowing us to see across isolated moments in different locations about the house as we fly across time over the coming weeks.)

*(**EMILY** writes in huge bold chalk:* Wuthering Heights *and* The Professor, *whilst* **CHARLOTTE** *gives* **ANNE** *notes:)*

CHARLOTTE. OK, first of all I *love* that your heroine is plain. *So* relatable –

ANNE. That's what I was going for!

CHARLOTTE. I've never seen a heroine *look* like that before, you know?

ANNE. Yes! Argh! I'm so happy you, like, *got* that –

CHARLOTTE. I just wonder about this title. Do you think something a little cleaner – like, how about just the name of your heroine?

*(**EMILY** writes* Agnes Grey *across the floor to join the other two titles.)*

ANNE. *Agnes Grey.*

CHARLOTTE. See, *that* might fit on the front cover.

(Time passes.)

*(**ANNE** and **EMILY**.)*

EMILY. *(Reading with gusto.)* "He seized and thrust her from the room; and returned muttering – 'I have no pity! I have no pity!' The more the worms writhe, the more I yearn to crush out their entrails!"

(**EMILY** *looks to* **ANNE** *expectantly –* **ANNE**, *who is looking deeply perturbed.*)

ANNE. Mm... I just... I don't think he's very likeable?

EMILY. What d'you mean?

ANNE. He just a bit... Murdery.

EMILY. Yeah, I don't think you're the right person to give me notes.

(*Time passes.*)

(**EMILY** *is giving* **CHARLOTTE** *notes.*)

It's just a case of tweaking.

CHARLOTTE. Really? Because these don't sound like tweaks.

EMILY. Honestly, they're small questions that will just tighten up the whole thing.

CHARLOTTE. I have no idea how to answer these.

EMILY. Yes you do.

CHARLOTTE. No, it's going in the bin. Don't want to do it anymore.

EMILY. (*Flatly.*) You're being dramatic.

CHARLOTTE. It's shit. It's going in the fire.

EMILY. Wait – !!

(*Time passes.*)

(**ANNE** *reads from* Agnes Grey *to* **CHARLOTTE** *and* **EMILY**, *who start furtively giggling as she speaks.*)

ANNE. (*Reading.*) "One glance he gave, one little smile at parting – it was but for a moment; but therein I read, or thought I read, a meaning that kindled in my heart a brighter flame of hope than had ever yet arisen."

(**ANNE** *looks up at her sisters, irritated.*)

What?

EMILY. Nothing.

CHARLOTTE. Just think we all know who *he's* based on.

(**CHARLOTTE** *and* **EMILY** *continue to laugh at an embarrassed* **ANNE** *over the next:*)

ANNE. What?! He is *NOT*!!

EMILY. *(Singsong.)* Anne and William sitting in a tree –

ANNE. You guys!! Stop it – it's *not funny*!

(Time passes.)

(**EMILY** *is frantically blowing out fire from* **CHARLOTTE***'s manuscript, whilst* **CHARLOTTE** *herself looks on terrified.*)

CHARLOTTE. Is it all there?

EMILY. You've lost the bottom right corner of the first eight chapters.

CHARLOTTE. NO!

EMILY. Well if you're going to throw it on the fire then it's going to get burned.

(Time passes.)

(**CHARLOTTE** *hands* **ANNE***'s volume back to her. Each hold their own manuscript.*)

CHARLOTTE. It is finished.

ANNE. You think?

CHARLOTTE. Not a word is wasted.

(**ANNE** *nods, beaming with pride.*)

ANNE. And yours?

EMILY. *Wuthering Heights* is done.

CHARLOTTE. As is *The Professor.*

EMILY. OK. Let's get them sent out.

> *(They each release their manuscripts, letting them fly up into the exterior male world of jackets above them where they disappear.)*
>
> *(A big collective intake of breath.)*
>
> *(Small white papers, rejections, start to rain down over them.)*
>
> *(With pace:)*

It's a 'no' from Jones and Co.

> *(Time passes.)*

ANNE. A 'no' from Samuel French.

> *(Time passes.)*

CHARLOTTE. A 'no' from Harper and Brothers.

EMILY. Where's the list of publishers?

> *(Time passes.)*

ANNE. Dear Misters Ellis, Currer and Acton Bell. Whilst we greatly enjoyed your work...

> *(Time passes.)*

EMILY. Regrettably we do not currently have the space...

> *(Time passes.)*

CHARLOTTE. For unknown authors at present...

> *(Time passes.)*

ANNE. We shall not give up. *I* believe in your writing.

CHARLOTTE. Thank you Mr Bell.

ANNE. No problem Mr Bell!

> *(Time passes.)*

> *(The papers start to slow to a trickle.)*

EMILY. A 'no' from Chapman and Hall.

> *(Time passes.)*

ANNE. Where's the list?

> *(Time passes.)*

CHARLOTTE. It is a 'no' from Le Monnier.

> *(Time passes.)*

EMILY. A 'no' from George Bell and Sons.

> *(Time passes.)*

ANNE. A 'no' from Macmillan.

> *(Time passes.)*

> *(The falling papers have come to a stop.)*

CHARLOTTE. Has anyone seen the post?

> *(Time passes.)*

> *(All remain still, looking upwards, waiting for a response. The floor thick with paper.)*

> *(Pause.)*

EMILY. Nothing.

> *(They each sit amid the paper rubbish.)*

(Pause.)

ANNE. What now?

*(**CHARLOTTE** sighs.)*

CHARLOTTE. Bed.

EMILY. Bed.

ANNE. I'll find the list of publishers.

CHARLOTTE. Anne, you should rest.

ANNE. I'll be right up.

(Her sisters leave.)

*(Left alone, **ANNE** picks up the list of publishers. She continues writing letters and sending out their manuscripts, writing by lamplight only as day turns into night, then back into the cold light of early morning.)*

*(Suddenly, out of the silence, a single white paper falls from above. **ANNE** watches it as it lands.)*

(She picks it up. She reads. And as she reads, she pauses – frozen.)

Emily.

(She looks up.)

Emily!

*(**EMILY** appears.)*

Thomas Newby...

*(**CHARLOTTE** appears.)*

The publisher Thomas Newby has – he has agreed to publish both *Agnes Grey* and *Wuthering Heights*.

EMILY. He hasn't.

ANNE. He has! It is written here.

> (**EMILY** *dashes over to* **ANNE** *to read the letter. She laughs disbelievingly.*)

EMILY. I can't believe it!

ANNE. *I* can't believe it!

> (*They embrace.*)

CHARLOTTE. *Agnes Grey* and *Wuthering Heights*.

> (**EMILY** *and* **ANNE** *look over to* **CHARLOTTE**.*)

ANNE. Oh Charlotte, I am so sorry.

> (**CHARLOTTE** *nods.*)

CHARLOTTE. They won't take *The Professor* (?)

ANNE. They've not given reasons as to why. I'm sure we could write back and convince them –

CHARLOTTE. No. No no.

This is good.

I'm happy for you.

This was the aim. Wasn't it?

To support each other.

One mask for all of us.

ANNE. Yeah… Alright.

> (**ANNE** *and* **EMILY** *leave* **CHARLOTTE** *to address the audience.*)

> (*She smiles tightly, trying to be gracious.*)

CHARLOTTE. Yep... Yes...

>   *(She fails.)*

Fuck that.

End Act One

ACT TWO

Scene One

"I Must Keep In Good Health And Not Die"

(Lights up.)

*(**CHARLOTTE** addresses the audience.)*

CHARLOTTE. One of the wonderful things about being a woman in 1846 is that you have absolutely bags of time to dedicate to random crap like putting dead peoples' hair into lockets or in my case, learning how to write with your eyes closed.

I was bullied at school for this, because I looked like a tit. But I always knew it would come in handy.

Our father's sight was worsening. His eyes had long been a problem and now it was obvious that the only thing that could save him from going completely blind was surgery. This would have to take place in Manchester and would demand a period of several weeks of recovery in a completely darkened room. Naturally it was our duty that one of us should go with him…

*(We are momentarily back in Haworth, with **ANNE** and **EMILY** present.)*

*(From this point on, only **CHARLOTTE** continues to wear her male jacket.)*

ANNE. I'll go. I could use the time to spend in prayer.

CHARLOTTE. *(To audience.)* You can really go off people, can't you?

*(To **ANNE**.)* No, you can't go. Neither of you can go. You both have work to do.

EMILY. What, editing? I'm not editing *Wuthering Heights*, they can like it or they can lump it. I also fear that *Mr Newby* is a swindler. For a publisher it seems that the actual act of publishing anything rarely crosses his mind.

ANNE. I also fear that's true.

CHARLOTTE. Oh nooo. No way! How could he let two such works of genius sit on a shelf! No. He shall publish imminently, I am sure of it. When's your publication date set for?

ANNE. We've not yet been given one.

CHARLOTTE. Oh shit, really? … Oh well, nevertheless.

*(To **EMILY**.)* You hate the city. *(To **ANNE**.)* And, forgive me Anne, but I believe I will be better at speaking with the doctors.

ANNE. You're probably right. *(Grimacing to **EMILY**.)* [They're] Creepy.

CHARLOTTE. That's settled then.

ANNE. Are you sure?

CHARLOTTE. Totally sure. I'll go and you can pray away back here.

ANNE. Well… Thanks.

EMILY. *(To **CHARLOTTE**.)* Good luck.

(**CHARLOTTE** *turns to leave.* **ANNE** *calls after her:)*

ANNE. Charlotte?

*(**CHARLOTTE** turns back.)*

Really. Thank you. I'm sure we'll find a publisher for *The Professor* soon.

CHARLOTTE. *(Tightly, attempted light.)* Mhm!

(The lights begin to darken around **CHARLOTTE** *so our focus is on her only. She speaks to the audience, with determination.)*

So I set off for Manchester with father, a pen and paper, to sit for weeks and weeks in the dark.

(She picks up a piece of chalk, ready to write. Across the stage, **ANNE** *remains dimly lit, alone and stood on a chair facing* **CHARLOTTE**.*)*

And that's when she came to me. My heroine.

*(**CHARLOTTE** creates a sign saying 'LIAR' and hangs it about* **ANNE**'s *neck over the next. The ensemble assume* **VOICE**'s *over the following)*

VOICE. Have you seen her?

She's pale.

She's plain.

So plain she hardly seems noticeable.

*(**CHARLOTTE** regards the image of* **ANNE** *stood on the chair with the sign about her neck and picks up her chalk. She watches her scene play out over the next, her lines spoken to herself, as though she is writing.)*

CHARLOTTE. *Jane Eyre.*

VOICE. I do not like the look of her.

There is nothing to like.

CHARLOTTE. *(To self.)* I am only asking permission to do what I *know* I am good at.

To be myself.

VOICE. Do all governesses remain alone forever?

CHARLOTTE. Yes.

VOICE. They are either too high or too low, which means they belong to no-one.

CHARLOTTE. *(To self.)* If I cannot work then I am nothing.

VOICE. They *think* they know everything, but have nothing to give, which makes them unloveable to everyone.

CHARLOTTE. *(To self.)* I will not be pushed aside. I will do whatever it takes to get into that room. I *will* join them. The Dickens's, the Thackeray's, The Byron's. I will get there. And when I get there I will show them just how wrong they were for trying to keep me out of it. I will surpass them all. I *will* –

> *(From her chair,* **ANNE** *voices a scene from* **CHARLOTTE***'s novel, distracting her. She picks up her chalk.)*

> *(Stood by* **ANNE** *is* **CHARLOTTE***'s creation,* **MR BROCKLEHURST** *– the head teacher from her novel.)*

MR BROCKLEHURST. Do you know where the wicked go after death?

ANNE. "They go to hell" –

CHARLOTTE. "Was my ready and orthodox answer".

MR BROCKLEHURST. And what is hell?

ANNE. "A pit full of fire".

MR BROCKLEHURST. And should you like to fall into that pit, and to be burning there for ever?

ANNE. "No, sir."

MR BROCKLEHURST. What must you do to avoid it?

CHARLOTTE. "I deliberated a moment: my answer, when it did come was objectionable" –

ANNE. "I must keep in good health and not die".

(**CHARLOTTE** *puts down her chalk, resolute.)*

CHARLOTTE. *(To self.)* I will live on forever.

Scene Two

"E.Y.R.E."

(**ANNE** *and* **EMILY** *sit working together when* **CHARLOTTE** *enters, breathless.*)

CHARLOTTE. I have excellent news!

ANNE. Charlotte!

CHARLOTTE. Hello. Is there wine?

EMILY. Where did you spring from?

CHARLOTTE. I *am* springy, aren't I?

ANNE. What's going on?

CHARLOTTE. The torture is over. My novel is finished.

ANNE. Oh my goodness!

CHARLOTTE. *(To audience.)* Papa was fine, by the way. Only took two men to hold him down; they slit his eyes open, stuck a couple leeches on his face to help with the inflammation and he was right as rain. Medicine is a marvel, truly. Nothing on what it took me to produce *Jane*, but – *(Noticing a bottle.)* Oh there *is* wine.

EMILY. It's not yet noon.

CHARLOTTE. We must toast!

ANNE. What has gotten into you?

CHARLOTTE. I am trying to tell you. My book!

EMILY. Yeah, what about your bloody book?

CHARLOTTE. It is being published.

ANNE. Oh my God!! Congratulations!

CHARLOTTE. I have a publisher!!

EMILY. Oh my God!!

(They all do a celebration group jump–up–and–down.)

CHARLOTTE. Thanks! Smith, Elder and Co. The big guns. Sure you've heard of them.

ANNE. This is insane!

*(**EMILY** pours them each a glass of wine.)*

EMILY. Wine wine wine!!

ANNE. Shh – Branwell –

EMILY. Oh yep. *(Quiet.) Wine wine wine!*

(They all cheers.)

CHARLOTTE. Eeee!!

ANNE & EMILY. Eeee!!

(They drink.)

CHARLOTTE. And, um, have you got a date for *Agnes Grey* and *Wuthering Heights* to come out yet?

ANNE. Not yet.

EMILY. Fucking Newby.

CHARLOTTE. Still?

EMILY. Nope.

ANNE. But never mind that, tell us about yours!! What – I mean, what's the title?

CHARLOTTE. *Jane Eyre*. But it's like 'e, y, r, e' which *is* a strange spelling, but I kind of like it. It's being published in two weeks.

ANNE. Two weeks?!

CHARLOTTE. Mad, right?!

ANNE. What's it about?

CHARLOTTE.   It is a wild and tempestuous tale of passionatc lovc bctwccn a courageous orphan and

(*To audience.*) the hottest man I have ever imagined

(*To* **EMILY**.*)* the brooding Mr Rochester.

ANNE. Brooding?

CHARLOTTE. Brooding, domineering, ferocious –

ANNE. He sounds awful.

CHARLOTTE & EMILY. Oh Anne.

ANNE. What?

EMILY. How do they meet?

CHARLOTTE.   So, she's working as a governess at his place –

(**EMILY** *looks over at* **ANNE**.*)*

ANNE. A governess?

CHARLOTTE. Yes.

ANNE. You wrote about a governess?

CHARLOTTE. Yes. What's the problem?

ANNE. What's she like, this governess?

CHARLOTTE. What woman is not Jane Eyre!

EMILY. Charlotte –

CHARLOTTE. She is both the spider and the web. She is muted, but wilful. Hers is a quiet, noble bid for freedom. A rebel slave. But she is as plain and as ordinary as you or I.

ANNE. I see.

EMILY. Sounds familiar.

CHARLOTTE. What? – Oh please, writers tread over the same materials all the time.

ANNE. You wrote the same character –

CHARLOTTE. *Jane* is nothing like *Agnes* –

ANNE. Must you write her as a governess then, when that is the very heart and soul of my book?

CHARLOTTE. As it is mine! The state of the governess so perfectly captures her outsider status –

ANNE. Yes –

CHARLOTTE. Her need to belong –

ANNE. Yes –

CHARLOTTE. Her societal oppression –

ANNE. Yes, yes –

CHARLOTTE. Stop saying 'yes' to everything!

ANNE. But I literally just wrote this!

CHARLOTTE. Erm, no you did not –

ANNE. You just read the very opinions you claim as your own!

CHARLOTTE. I lived it too –

ANNE. Captured in a character, who dare I say it sounds a lot –

CHARLOTTE. Do *not* –

ANNE. Like me!

CHARLOTTE. Wow Anne, that is quite narcissistic.

ANNE. You *know* it's my work!

CHARLOTTE. Read it, you'll see that it's not.

ANNE. It does not matter if I do or do not, it's being published anyway.

CHARLOTTE. I held the pen. I conjured the thoughts. *I* drew on *my* experiences –

ANNE. Yes and now your novel will beat mine to the press and *I* will look like a fraud!

CHARLOTTE. I am telling you, the novels are different. Could not be more different.

Mine is strange and gothic and intense. Yours is... Realistic.

ANNE. Ha! So you will make a fairytale out of the very predicament I desire to change! Change by holding a mirror to the life and so exposing its ugliness.

CHARLOTTE. Well you can still do that. Sounds fun. I fail to see the problem.

ANNE. If you do this – if you take a story so similar in structure and character and publish just before mine, then you *know Agnes Grey* will not receive half the attention it deserves.

CHARLOTTE. Yet if I publish second to you then *Jane Eyre* will not receive half the attention it deserves. We both had experience of being governesses, I have just as much right over the story as you.

ANNE. Please. Just wait until mine is released first.

CHARLOTTE. *If* it is released at all.

EMILY. Charlotte!

CHARLOTTE. I don't know why you are being so hostile towards my success. It's one mask for all three of us, remember?

ANNE. No. When we all submitted our own stories, then it was a mutual support. *This* is competition.

CHARLOTTE. Competition! *(Deeply sarcastic.)* Oh I forgot, the enemy of woman kind.

ANNE. You are actively pitting my story against yours.

CHARLOTTE. Why? Why is there not room for both? Look at all this room! Shelves and shelves of it. Look here!

> *(She points to a book shelf, along a row of titles.)*

Murder most foul, murder most foul, story about a king, story about a king, story about another king, war, war, war... *Same fucking subject matter.*

ANNE. It is *different* with women's stories. You know that! We're already a bloody sub-genre! Once one woman has written about her experiences that tread new ground and it manages to break through, then that becomes the one and only narrative permitted. The spaces for women are *limited* –

CHARLOTTE. But we are not women, are we?

ANNE. We are writing women.

CHARLOTTE. As men.

ANNE. Please.

> Let me have this. You know how I have worked for this. I have spent five years –

CHARLOTTE. No. You're not worried that there are two novels with the same subject matter. You're worried that mine is better.

ANNE. Charlotte!

CHARLOTTE. But I think what, in time, you will truly find hard to bear, is that you were willing to squash our ideals of giving voice to a whole generation of other women in service to your own vanity. You know Anne... It should not be *who* writes our story, but that it was written. That it was written and at least one of our voices will be given the platform.

ANNE. Oh fuck you.

> *(**ANNE** exits.)*

CHARLOTTE. Nice argument!

(CHARLOTTE turns to EMILY.)

EMILY. Congratulations.

(She follows after ANNE.)

CHARLOTTE. Oh, not you too –

(Calling.) Emily!

(She's cut off by the next scene.)

Scene Three

"Ladylike Tricks"

(Grandiose, whirling music plays as critics circle the stage. They address one another in a gentlemen's club, making a conversation out of their reviews. They are a mixture of genders, but all presenting as men.)

(Whilst they 'chat', all smoke from pipes which puff excessively so that as the scene progresses **CHARLOTTE** *and* **ANNE** *become increasingly cloaked in mist and chocked on it.)*

WESTMINSTER REVIEW. "The best novel of the season!"

CHARLOTTE. The Westminster Review is in!!

THE ATLAS. "This is not merely a work of great promise. It is one of absolute performance"

CHARLOTTE. Ah! *The Atlas*! Have you read *The Atlas*?!

ANNE. Not yet.

CHARLOTTE. What's the matter?

ANNE. *Agnes Grey* and *Wuthering Heights* are being sent to the printers.

CHARLOTTE. But that is good news? Finally!

ANNE. *(Unconvincing.)* Yes. Yes, it is very exciting.

GEORGE HENRY LEWES. "After laughing over *The Bachelor of the Albany*, we wept over *Jane Eyre* –"

CRITIC. A masterpiece!

QUARTERLY. Remarkable!

THOMAS REID. *Jane Eyre* fever grips the nation!

GEORGE HENRY LEWES. – This, indeed, is a book after our own heart; and, if its merits have not forced it into notice by the time this paper comes before our readers, let us, in all earnestness, bid them not to lose a day in sending for it...

> *(***CHARLOTTE*** dons her most 'masculine' stance – really trying to live and breath the role.)*

CHARLOTTE. *(A public response.)* Thank you. Thank you very much my fellow... Lads. This is a real honour and –

GEORGE HENRY LEWES. *(Continued, interrupting.)* The writer is evidently a woman, and, unless deceived, new to the world of literature.'

CHARLOTTE. S'cuse me?

THACKERAY. *(Agreeing with* **LEWES***.)* Who the author can be I can't guess – if a woman, she knows her language better than most ladies do, or has had a 'classical' education...

CHARLOTTE. Thackeray?!

> *(***THACKERAY*** shrugs at her. ***CHARLOTTE*** is increasingly torn by trying to combat every critics opinion:)*

THACKERAY. I don't know why I tell you this but that I have been exceedingly moved and pleased by *Jane Eyre* –

CHARLOTTE. Thank you –

THACKERAY. – It is a woman's writing, but whose?

CHARLOTTE. How do they all know?!

> *(She continues to read the press. ***ANNE*** also reads, trying to bat away the thickening smoke clouds.)*

THE CHRISTIAN REMEMBRANCER. "The book's masculine hardness, coarseness, and freedom of expression are entirely inappropriate for a female author."

CHARLOTTE. *(Affronted.) Alright –*

WESTMINSTER REVIEW. Agreed.

FONBLANQUE. Thoroughly rude and uncultivated.

THE ERA. No woman could have possibly written such vulgarity.

LONDON MAGAZINE. No woman under thirty ought to open it!

ELIZABETH RIGBY. If indeed this novel *has* been written by a woman, then she has clearly long forfeited the society of her own sex!

> *(Exhausted, **CHARLOTTE** leans further into her most 'masculine' stance. She speaks with venom.)*

CHARLOTTE. *(Publicly.)* Sorry – sorry – sorry – EXCUSE ME!

> *(The critics turn to **CHARLOTTE**.)*

Alright. First of all, yes, I've tried to be enigmatical on the subject, but I'm quite obviously a bloke.

> *(Murmurs of agreement/disagreement from the critics.)*

Secondly! It's none of your fucking business.

> *(More shocked murmurs from the critics. **CHARLOTTE** looks increasingly fraught by the increased attention, making her go further on the petulant defensive.)*

And *thirdly*! I know for a fact that Rousseau wears a corset, Dickens gives off massive housewife energy, and if Tennyson's not actually a woman I'll eat my cravat. So I suggest you look elsewhere.

(The critics dissipate to circle the edges of the space in a waft of tittering at this last to watch the following. **CHARLOTTE** *exhales, with relief at getting them momentarily off her back. The music fades with their departure. The smoke begins to evaporate.)*

*(***CHARLOTTE*** *begins to write frantically. We are now in her bedroom.)*

*(***ANNE*** *appears in the doorway.)*

ANNE. Letter for you.

CHARLOTTE. Oh. Thanks.

*(***ANNE*** *lingers as* **CHARLOTTE** *remains bent over her work, hiding her emotion.)*

ANNE. You alright?

CHARLOTTE. Oh. Yes. Yep, I'm fine. Just trying to keep up with all the... All my correspondence.

ANNE. Sorry, I'll um [go] –

CHARLOTTE. No! Please. Would – would you stay?

*(***ANNE*** *nods. She enters the room, ready to listen.)*

I just don't know *how* they seem to know I'm not a man.

(With forced bravado.) I suppose men aren't allowed to write women that well! Am I right?

ANNE. Um. Sure.

CHARLOTTE. It just, it doesn't seem fair... You know?

*(***ANNE*** *sits – a mother to a distressed child.)*

I mean, you can do everything right. You can work and work and work... You – you can change your name, you can get a publisher, you can have a hit, you can have the whole goddamn country buy your book and it is *still* not enough.

Just – if someone would just tell me what I can do!

I am trying so hard.

Just please.

Please tell me what I can do to be enough.

ANNE. *(Gently.)* You're enough for me.

CHARLOTTE. I will show them you know. I will get there.

ANNE. You already are there. This is it! It's been written.

CHARLOTTE. But not accepted.

ANNE. I think your readers would disagree.

CHARLOTTE. But not the critics. Not the authors. Not the gatekeepers.

ANNE. That's not strictly true.

CHARLOTTE. It *is* true!

ANNE. Forget about reviews. What's worrying is how you're responding.

CHARLOTTE. You don't think I should defend myself?

ANNE. No, not at all. But, look at you, it's becoming an obsession. You're spending more time writing about what people are writing about you than writing anything else!

And – I don't know – it feels like you're playing a role.

CHARLOTTE. That was your idea.

ANNE. I only suggested pseudonyms. Not characters.

CHARLOTTE. But you've seen the responses! If they read the work and bclicvc I am a man, they pronounce it a masterpiece. If they read the work and even so much as *suspect* that I am a woman, they denounce it as inappropriate. Lustful.

ANNE. Believe me I understand. It is unfair. And I support you doing whatever necessary to protect what you have created. For it to be seen as the work of an *author*, not a woman. But at the moment, you are giving up Charlotte Brontë for Currer Bell – this *idea* you have of being a man. When really you only ever wanted the world to see that the two could exist together. In everyone. That neither men nor women should be told how to be. Look – look at our brother! How he suffers for the whole of society dictating what 'masculinity' requires from him. How it consumes him, the conflict within himself that he must be part of the 'hard sex', when really he is sensitive and poetic and kind –

CHARLOTTE. He is spoiled and entitled.

ANNE. He is a victim, just as much as we are. He is behaving how he has been taught he should behave. And you know how it is destroying him. I fear for him Charlotte – if he carries on this way I don't think he can survive much longer.

CHARLOTTE. Oh for fucks sake, he doesn't even know we've been writing so we can protect his precious ego. I am not about to have sympathy for bloody Branwell right now. I have my own battles.

ANNE. You don't mean that.

CHARLOTTE. Yes, I do.

ANNE. No, you don't.

CHARLOTTE. Yes, I do.

ANNE. No, you don't.

CHARLOTTE. Stop it yes I do times a thousand.

(**ANNE** *grins.*)

ANNE. Who's the letter from?

CHARLOTTE. Oh. George Smith.

ANNE. He writes a lot (?)

CHARLOTTE. He's my publisher.

ANNE. Even so... You enjoy writing to him?

CHARLOTTE. (*Defensive, somewhat coy.*) He writes well.

(**ANNE** *smiles.*)

ANNE. High praise indeed Mr Bell.

(**CHARLOTTE** *fails to suppress something of a grin. She keep her eyes on the floor, awkward.*)

CHARLOTTE. We're actually very friendly.

ANNE. (*Teasing.*) You *are* his most famous client.

CHARLOTTE. (*Bashful.*) No I'm not...

ANNE. You are!

CHARLOTTE. Stop it.

ANNE. You're *famous.*

CHARLOTTE. (*Enjoying being teased.*) Anne, stop it.

ANNE. Does Emily know?

CHARLOTTE. No! Do *not* tell Emily.

ANNE. (*Entertained.*) Fair enough.

CHARLOTTE. Anyway there's nothing to tell. He doesn't even know that I'm a woman.

(**CHARLOTTE** *looks at her sister, her smile gone.*)

(Small.) It's why he continues to write.

ANNE. You never know.

(Small pause.)

CHARLOTTE. You're being nice to me.

ANNE. Ha.

CHARLOTTE. After I was such a dick.

ANNE. You're always a dick.

CHARLOTTE. I'm not *always* a dick.

ANNE. You are *always* a dick.

CHARLOTTE. But you're letting me off...?

ANNE. Little bit.

CHARLOTTE. I'm sorry about *Agnes Grey*.

ANNE. I try not to pay attention. The reviews have been bad I gather?

CHARLOTTE. Um –

WEEKLY NEWS. "*Agnes Grey* is a tale well worth the writing and the reading. The heroine is a sort of younger sister to *Jane Eyre*... But inferior to her in every way."

THE ATLAS. "It leaves no painful impression on the mind – some may think it leaves no impression at all."

ANNE. I – I – I don't care.

CHARLOTTE. Really?

ANNE. I don't care about other people. *Your* opinion is what matters to me.

CHARLOTTE. God I couldn't not listen to what people were saying about me.

*(**ANNE** looks at her pointedly.)*

And, you know, *same*! Your opinion's great. Really great. I really value your opinion.

ANNE. *(Dryly.)* Thanks Charlotte.

CHARLOTTE. So you really don't blame me?

ANNE. No, you were right. They were different stories. You know, everyone else can pit us against each other Charlotte. It doesn't mean we have to.

CHARLOTTE. That's sweet Anne... It's bollocks, but sweet.

ANNE. Ha! Why's it bollocks?

CHARLOTTE. Come on – tell me my success doesn't make you want to better me.

Overwrite me.

> *(**ANNE** smiles.)*

ANNE. No comment.

CHARLOTTE. Ha! There! You see!

ANNE. I don't like where this is going –

CHARLOTTE. You might not like it, but I *bet* your next novel will be better –

ANNE. *(Playing, sarcastic.)* And you'll take the credit.

CHARLOTTE. No, I'll write a better novel.

ANNE. Theeere she is.

> *(**CHARLOTTE** smiles.)*

> *(**ANNE** smiles back, gives her hand a squeeze.)*

Now defend what you've made. Properly.

CHARLOTTE. And you? Are you working on something?

ANNE. I am.

CHARLOTTE. What – what's it about?

    *(**ANNE** smiles, mischievously.)*

ANNE. *(Playfully echoing her sister.)* I might go write in my room.

CHARLOTTE. Oh, come on! *(Laughingly.)* Just tell me a –

    (They're interrupted by a rumble of drums starting up from above them, within the dome of jackets.)

    (Both jump. They look upward towards the sound, afraid and knowing exactly who is creating the noise.)

*(To **ANNE**, protectively.)* Go.

Scene Four

"The Tenant of Wildfell Hall"

(The rumble of drums continues.)

*(**BRANWELL** and **EMILY** appear; **EMILY** trying to control her drunk and aggressive brother. The waspish humour and the spark has visibly drained from him, leaving only the anger and hurt.)*

CHARLOTTE. *(To audience.)* I may have started *Jane Eyre* in complete darkness, but Anne wrote the whole of *The Tenant of Wildfell Hall* in a house that was turning into a battlefield.

> *(**ANNE** picks up her chalk and observes **EMILY** and **BRANWELL**. She starts to write.)*

It was a terrifying book. *Truly* terrifying, because she had spun it from reality. She took inspiration not just from our own brother, but women everywhere living under the threat of violence. She wrote for them with a fire and fury I had not seen before – not just in her, *but in fiction*. Anywhere.

> *(**BRANWELL** relents, collapsing into **EMILY**'s arms, coughing blood. She cradles him.)*

She took for her heroine a scorned woman, a mother no less, who flees an abusive marriage in order to save her son from the toxic behaviour of her husband.

She has to steal, lie, hide in order to survive. She lives, fugitive, in an abandoned tower of an old manor house –

EMILY. Branwell's started coughing blood.

(**CHARLOTTE** *tries to ignore her. She enjoys the rivalry of the next:*)

CHARLOTTE. Oh I saw what she was doing. She was pointing at me! Because all of this determination does not lead her into the arms of a fit-but-problematic saviour. She and only she is the hero of her story.

EMILY. Charlotte?

CHARLOTTE. She was setting an example.

Because the *whole book*, in fact, was strewn with different accounts of violence, clues to domestic abuse and passages to escape.

(**ANNE** *writes from tenant, watching her siblings.*)

ANNE. "The door being now free, Milicent attempted to make her escape from the scene of her husband's disgrace; but he called her back, and insisted upon her coming to him".

(**EMILY** *and* **BRANWELL** *voice the characters Milicent and Ralph, whilst also remaining as themselves.*)

EMILY. "What do you want Ralph?"

ANNE. "Murmured she, reluctantly approaching him".

(**EMILY** *does so. They play out the narrated actions over the next:*)

BRANWELL. "I want to know what's the matter with you,"

ANNE. "said he, pulling her on to his knee like a child"

(**EMILY** *recoils from him, pained at his threatening behaviour.*)

BRANWELL. "What are you crying for, Milicent? – Tell me!'

EMILY. "I'm not crying."

BRANWELL. "You are,"

ANNE. "persisted he, rudely pulling her hands from her face."

BRANWELL. "How dare you tell such a lie!"

EMILY. "I'm not crying now,"

ANNE. "pleaded she."

BRANWELL. "But you have been, and just this minute too; and I will know what for. Come, now, you shall tell me!"

EMILY. "Do let me alone, Ralph! Remember, we are not at home."

> (**EMILY** *forcefully disengages herself from her brother and, shaken, she staggers away from him to* **CHARLOTTE.**)

CHARLOTTE. We're not at home.

We are not at home.

EMILY. No.

> (*Over the next a distraught* **BRANWELL** *seeks help from the male jackets above, pulling one down towards him. He rips the jacket off its rope, fashioning himself a noose.*)

CHARLOTTE. (*To audience.*) And while her heroine, by the end, finds financial freedom, falls in love with a good man and succeeds in taking ownership over her own story...

> (**BRANWELL** *places the noose about his neck.*)

... Her tormentor destroys himself.

> (*Just as he strings himself up,* **EMILY** *catches him.*)

EMILY. STOP!

> (**BRANWELL** *collapses to the floor in tears as*
> **EMILY** *comforts him.*)

> (*The roll of drums from above stops.*)

CHARLOTTE. The moment it hit the press the reviews
flew in.

> (*The* **CRITICS** *reappear with their cigars, in*
> *conversation with each other.* **CHARLOTTE**
> *continues to speak directly to the audience.*)

CRITIC 1. It is disgusting, revolting, brutal and unwomanly.

> (*Spent from writing,* **ANNE** *looks up from her*
> *work, horrified at the reaction it has caused.*)

CHARLOTTE. I read each and every one.

NORTH AMERICAN REVIEW. Mr Acton Bell brings the
reader into the closest proximity with naked vice, and
there are conversations such as we had hoped to never
to see printed in English.

CHARLOTTE. It was a sensation.

LITERARY WORLD. Can this sort of half–civilisation, half
beautification, be characteristic of English society?

CHARLOTTE. With each controversial review, sales went
up and up. Just six weeks and the first edition was
already sold out.

MAY SINCLAIR. The slamming of Helen Huntingdon's
door against her husband reverberates through all
England.

> (**ANNE** *stands, responding to the criticism,*
> *speaking either to* **EMILY** *or to herself.*
> **CHARLOTTE** *remains focused solely on what*
> *the critics say.*)

ANNE. I will not stop writing until there is change.

THE ATHENAEUM. These Bells brothers, if indeed they are brothers, must be warned against their fancy for dwelling upon what is disagreeable.

ANNE. I will not stop until women can leave their husbands without it being *theft*.

CRITIC 2. Utterly unbelievable! Mr Acton Bell –

CRITIC 1. Or should we say *Miss* –

CRITIC 2. Seems hell bent on ripping apart the established rules of society in a colourful drama which we find little more than cheap,

THE SPECTATOR. Crude,

THE ANTHENAEUM. Vulgar,

CRITIC 2. Melodrama. Not fit for women's eyes –

CHARLOTTE. *(To* **CRITICS**.*)* STOP!! *STOP!!*

ANNE. *(Quietly, to herself.)* I will not stop.

> *(**CHARLOTTE** looks both surprised and concerned at her sister's resolve.)*
>
> *(The critics disappear, leaving their clouds of cigar smoke.)*
>
> *(**GEORGE SMITH** enters.)*

CHARLOTTE. George!

> *(He hands her a letter.)*

GEORGE. Dear Mr Bell.

I hope this finds you in good health. Just a little note to ask... What the piss is going on?!

It seems a new book by *our* esteemed author Mr C. Bell – i.e. *you* – is simply flying off the shelves, which

– though it's rather grotesque in it's subject matter – would all be fine and dandy if it weren't for the fact that you had so kindly, so generously, so *contractually*, agreed to publish your next work of fiction with *us*.

Would be marvellous if you could reply post haste before we send a legal shit storm your way.

Yours sincerely, George Smith.

> (**GEORGE** *exits, leaving* **CHARLOTTE** *with her letter.*)

Scene Five

"There's Been A Mix Up"

(**EMILY** and **ANNE** in the kitchen, baking an enormous pie and finding it hilarious.)

(**CHARLOTTE** enters with the letter in hand, infuriated.)

ANNE. Charlotte!

EMILY. Look, we're making a massive pork pie to celebrate Anne's officially becoming the biggest fucking superstar of all time!

ANNE. *(Bashful, to* **EMILY***.)* Stop it –

EMILY. Best seller!

ANNE. *(To* **CHARLOTTE***.)* Look! It's shaped like an actual star!

EMILY. Nothing says 'success' like a star made out of pork!

CHARLOTTE. What the fuck have you done?

ANNE. Alright, it's not that bad.

CHARLOTTE. There's been a mix up. Your *publisher* has tried to pass off that novel of yours under *my* name.

ANNE. What?

CHARLOTTE. He's trying to boost his sales in America by pretending that *The Tenant of Wildfell Hall* has been written by the author of *Jane Eyre* –

ANNE. Well – what – I didn't have anything to do with it!

CHARLOTTE. And now your ugly little book is hurting *my* reputation –

EMILY. Hold on!

CHARLOTTE. Smith, Elder and Co. have first refusal on my next two novels.

This looks like I have deceived them.

EMILY. Just write and explain Newby's made a mistake. The tit.

CHARLOTTE. And wait days on end with people thinking *that book* belongs to Currer Bell?!

ANNE. What do you mean 'that book'?

EMILY. Jesus Charlotte, people are confusing us 'Bells' all the time. Half the nation believes we are one person. We're a myth mate, nothing more.

ANNE. I – I – I thought you would be proud.

CHARLOTTE. Proud?! You've gutted your own family for a bit of fiction.

ANNE. What? No, I haven't –

CHARLOTTE. As if it's not painful enough to watch Branwell demonise himself to the point of destruction, you now string him out before the whole of England. It's not right.

ANNE. But, but no–one even knows it's me!

EMILY. Oh but that's no longer the point Anne. She's threatened by you now, so she's cheating.

CHARLOTTE. Excuse me?

EMILY. You *know* you don't believe what you're saying. As if this is about your sudden concern for Branwell.

CHARLOTTE. It is!

EMILY. Can you not just be happy for her that's it's successful? You can't make room can you?

CHARLOTTE. It's not *me* not making room, it's your bloody publisher!

EMILY. So what! Who cares who it gets credited to! They're not *our* names anyway. The important thing is that it's being read. Right? Isn't that what you said?

CHARLOTTE. This is different. You can't write this shit! People will – they *are* – out for you –

ANNE. I don't want to know what they're saying.

(*To* **EMILY**.) You said it's not doing any worse than *Wuthering Heights* or *Jane Eyre*.

EMILY. It's not.

CHARLOTTE. Oh yes it is! There's no ghosts or mad women to blame in this one, just clandestine violence and alcohol. You have literally attacked two of the cultural pillars of British society.

EMILY. So what? It's visionary.

CHARLOTTE. It's splashy and immature.

ANNE. (*Winded.*) What?

CHARLOTTE. There is a difference between forward thinking and downright scandalous. If you were to ever be found out, it would *ruin* you –

EMILY. Who says we're going to be found out?

CHARLOTTE. I'm talking to Anne –

EMILY. And I'm talking to you! So you want the world to catch up with your views, but only yours, is that it? That's not progress Charlotte, that's narcissism.

CHARLOTTE. No, this is about protecting our reputations. All of them.

EMILY. You mean our pseudonyms reputations. This isn't about propriety, it's about pride. Don't knock your sister's work and pretend like you're doing her a favour.

One mask for all three of us, wasn't it? One mask to help all of our voices get heard –

CHARLOTTE. That is how it *started* –

EMILY. Until your voice became the loudest. And you want to keep it that way.

CHARLOTTE. No, I am *trying* to protect us.

EMILY. Please.

CHARLOTTE. *(To* **ANNE**.*)* Really, I am. I'm going to London this afternoon.

EMILY. What the *fuck*?!

CHARLOTTE. I am going to tell my publishers what has happened in person.

EMILY. You can't do that, you'll expose all of us!

CHARLOTTE. I will only tell George. I cannot have him thinking I broke my contract.

EMILY. If you dare –

CHARLOTTE. *(To* **ANNE**.*)* I would appreciate it if you came with me to explain.

EMILY. Anne. You don't have to –

ANNE. I – I don't know –

CHARLOTTE. It should be the two of us together. A united front.

ANNE. Yes – Yeah –

CHARLOTTE. We can retain our anonymity to everyone but our publishers.

EMILY. You will be inviting the outside world in –

CHARLOTTE. They're already in!

EMILY. You know that's not true. Not for me, not for her –

CHARLOTTE. This is just as much for her sake as it is for mine. She ought to be able to claim her work, if she's going to stand by it.

EMILY. Please, that's hardly –

ANNE. Enough!

I'll go.

EMILY. Anne. Really?

ANNE. It's my work that's being pirated… It's time I claimed it.

I believe in it, after all. I should be able to defend what I've put on the page in person.

CHARLOTTE. Yes, exactly.

ANNE. And you mean it? That we go together, that we're still a united front? I know between ourselves, as writers, we might differ. But out there you'll still be my sister, won't you?

CHARLOTTE. Of course. I promise.

ANNE. OK. OK then… I'll go get my things.

(**EMILY** *turns to* **CHARLOTTE**.)

EMILY. You know you're becoming just like the bullies you so admire.

(**ANNE** *exits*. **EMILY** *follows her.*)

(**CHARLOTTE** *looks to the audience.*)

CHARLOTTE. In other words, I was winning.

End Act Two

(*Blackout.*)

ACT THREE

Scene One

"London, Euston"

(Lights up.)

*(**CHARLOTTE** and **ANNE** get into a horse drawn carriage. **CHARLOTTE** addresses the audience.)*

CHARLOTTE.   So, the carriage ride to London was seventeen hours.

We weren't talking...

*(**CHARLOTTE** looks to **ANNE**, who is staring out of the window.)*

(To audience.) I think she's fine.

She seems fine...

*(To **ANNE**.)* You alright?

ANNE. *(Deeply irritated.)* I'm *fine*.

*(**CHARLOTTE** shoots a terrified look at the audience.)*

CHARLOTTE. *(To audience.)* Let me tell you, seventeen hours is a very long fucking time.

DRIVER. Next stop London, Euston!

CHARLOTTE. Oh thank God.

> *(They step off the carriage and out onto the city street.)*

(To audience.) London!

The place each of us had eviscerated in fiction as a cesspool of corruption, smog and sin was, in reality, just as much of a shithole as I'd imagined.

We stayed in some godforsaken B&B, used mostly by other authors summoned to the city by their publishers and news hounds. I saw a real life prostitute for the first time in my life, got a rash from the bed sheets, drunk a quart of brandy to conk myself out for the night then awoke the next morning for what I was sure might be the most momentous day of my life. The day I would reveal myself to the man who had made all of my good fortune, my – or Currer's – fame possible... Who, it seemed from his letters, really respected me.

Scene Two

"Oh Shit"

(Split scene. **CHARLOTTE** *and* **ANNE** *knock on the doors of their respective publishers:* **MR GEORGE SMITH** *and* **THOMAS NEWBY**.*)*

CHARLOTTE. Mr George Smith?

GEORGE. May I help you?

ANNE. Mr Thomas Newby?

NEWBY. Who's asking?

CHARLOTTE. My name is Charlotte Brontë.

GEORGE. Mr Bell's secretary! All the way from Yorkshire?!

CHARLOTTE. Yes! And this is my sister –

ANNE. Anne Brontë.

NEWBY. Oh fuck. From behind the Ship and Shovel?

GEORGE. Delightful!

ANNE. S'cuse me?

NEWBY. Oh. Never mind.

GEORGE. So good to finally meet you.

CHARLOTTE. Now –

ANNE. I have something of a confession to make –

CHARLOTTE. I am – I am also Currer Bell himself. Um. What I mean to say is –

ANNE. My pen name is Acton Bell –

CHARLOTTE. But the author of your novels is –

ANNE. In fact –

CHARLOTTE. Me.

GEORGE. Good Lord.

NEWBY. Oh shit.

CHARLOTTE. I have evidence by way of handwriting samples and the letters we have passed between each other.

ANNE. Here –

> *(They each pass their letters over to their respected publishers.)*

GEORGE. This is – this is unbelievable!

NEWBY. Bullshit.

ANNE. Um. I assure you it is not.

CHARLOTTE. It's there in writing –

GEORGE. No! No, dear lady, I obviously believe you. What I mean to say is, this is – this is quite fantastical! An honour!

NEWBY. Women don't write like that.

CHARLOTTE. Seriously?!

GEORGE. *(Elated.)* The author of *Jane Eyre* – a woman!

CHARLOTTE. I am! I am a woman!

GEORGE. By Jove! I am quite speechless!

ANNE. I don't know what to say to that –

CHARLOTTE. I hope you are not disappointed?

GEORGE. Disappointed?! Good lord no!

NEWBY. The fuck am I supposed to do about this –

GEORGE. Such a friendship we have had! Such intimate confidences –

CHARLOTTE. I hope you do not regret them –

GEORGE. I – I do not!

ANNE. You *know* I am the author of *The Tenant of Wildfell Hall*, yet you knowingly deceived the public and tried to pass off my novel under my sister's name.

CHARLOTTE. I, for one, spoke from the heart. I have not deceived you in that and I have not betrayed our contract. It was a mistake on my sister's publisher Newby's behalf.

GEORGE. The scoundrel!

NEWBY. For God's sake...

GEORGE. Well this is a great comfort, to be sure. *(To* **ANNE.***)* No offence –

ANNE. Nevertheless. Smith, Elder and Co. are aware and I suggest you correct the error before your *favour* does us both financial harm.

NEWBY. Right –

GEORGE. You are. Um. Breath-taking –

CHARLOTTE. Oh!

GEORGE. – that you are here, I mean.

CHARLOTTE. Oh.

GEORGE. The whole of London shall be a buzz –

ANNE. Now wait.

NEWBY. Oh what else?

ANNE. Our third 'brother', Ellis Bell demands that we retain our anonymity.

GEORGE. I see.

NEWBY. Sure... Mum's the word...

GEORGE. But still. To have come all this way and not experience the very best of society! Even if I cannot introduce you to the world as Currer Bell, at least allow me to show you what literary London has to offer Charlotte Brontë.

CHARLOTTE. Really?

GEORGE. Really –

> (**GEORGE** *offers an arm to* **CHARLOTTE**. *She goes to take it, delighted.*)

NEWBY. But Miss Brontë you should know – you two carry on like this and someone's going to find out who you really are. And when they do this whole little kerfuffle will look like nothing. This is a man's game. And I'm not so sure you're the type to be able to handle it.

GEORGE. It's where you belong.

> (*He leads* **CHARLOTTE** *out of his office –* **ANNE** *following.*)

Scene Three

"The Room"

CHARLOTTE. When I spent all those years fantasising about what it would really *mean* to be 'in the room', I was always thinking metaphorically. Only when Anne and I got to London did I see that that position of power and influence, that symbolic seat of those lofty minds who shaped the cultural consciousness was – for the most part – an actual room. Apparently finding one's way to this Mount Olympus of mine was as simple as gaining access to what was quite literally known as a 'member's club'. To get there one didn't really need to write great novels, or conjure new ways of thinking, or discover anything much. One simply needed to be on the arm of a rich white bloke.

Course, I didn't acknowledge this at the time. At the time it was... Heaven...

(They enter the club, full of the great and the good.)

(All dance to "The Safety Dance" by Men Without Hats.)

GEORGE. Now *this* is London!

*(**CHARLOTTE** and **GEORGE** join the dance. **ANNE** lingers back.)*

(The music fades.)

CHARLOTTE. Fuck me is that Dickens?!

GEORGE. Leaves home to avoid his wife. Finds himself here dodging his mistress.

CHARLOTTE. Noooo.

GEORGE. Don't get me started.

CHARLOTTE. Tell me everything!

GEORGE. But first, may I have this dance?

CHARLOTTE. Me?

(To audience.) Sorry. But you know those moments when you just feel such happiness or panic or elation or blind fear and you go all fizzy and all you can really hear is white noise and if anyone was to ask you later what happened you wouldn't really fully honestly remember?

GEORGE. Yes. You.

> *(Brief tinnitus style white noise blocks out all other sound as* **GEORGE** *leans in again, still speaking to* **CHARLOTTE**.*)*

CHARLOTTE. *(To audience.)* This was one of those moments.

(To **GEORGE**.*)* Um, yeah. OK. I would be honoured.

> *(They dance.)*

You know, Mr Smith, you were a terrific arsehole in your letter.

GEORGE. Forgive me, Miss Brontë, my pride was wounded –

CHARLOTTE. Oh my God you sound like an Austen novel –

GEORGE. I know you well enough to realise that isn't a compliment.

CHARLOTTE. Sorry, I know I can be a dick, I can't help it, it's like word vomit –

GEORGE. No, no you may examine me all you like. For all the world is now yours to examine and either find wanting or to your taste. After all, he who holds the pen has the power –

(Second of the same tinnitus white noise again.)

CHARLOTTE. *(To audience.)* Sorry. Again, sorry. But *wow* –

*(Back to **GEORGE**.)* Is it me or are people looking?

GEORGE. I believe rumours have already started of your true identity –

CHARLOTTE. When?! How?!

GEORGE. This is London, people have a sixth sense for smelling out stars –

CHARLOTTE. That makes no sense!

GEORGE. They are looks of admiration.

CHARLOTTE. You flatter me.

GEORGE. I intend to.

CHARLOTTE. Sorry – I'm just – I can't believe I'm really here. This doesn't feel real.

GEORGE. Don't worry. I've got you.

*(Their dance is interrupted by a tap on **CHARLOTTE**'s shoulder.)*

ANNE. Um, Charlotte?

CHARLOTTE. Oh god – what is it?

ANNE. I want to go home.

CHARLOTTE. *(To **GEORGE**.)* Please, excuse me one moment...

*(To **ANNE**.)* Um. Are you bloody bonkers?

ANNE. I don't like it here.

CHARLOTTE. How?! There is music. There is food. There is Charles Dickens chowing down on a pickled egg and hiding behind a pot plant. What's not to love?

ANNE. This isn't why we came.

CHARLOTTE. Look. I've dreamed of being here my whole life. Standing shoulder to shoulder with these people. And –

> *(She glances warily over at **GEORGE** and lowers her voice.)*

And, now it's finally happening I want to just enjoy it. Will you let me just enjoy it?

ANNE. Fine. You do you. I'll be hiding in the ladies loos.

CHARLOTTE. Well knock yourself out. They have plumbing here.

> *(**CHARLOTTE** turns back to find **GEORGE**, who is speaking with his partner **SMITH WILLIAMS**.)*

SMITH. So it's true. Currer Bell really is a woman.

GEORGE. Indeed she is... Miss Charlotte Brontë.

> *(Hearing her name, **CHARLOTTE** lingers back.)*

SMITH. And the pair of you were dancing I see.

GEORGE. Indeed we were.

SMITH. Could this become more than a professional relationship?

> *(**CHARLOTTE** leans in.)*

GEORGE. Christ no. Who would have thought. The infamous Currer Bell is some loud four-eyed squat from Yorkshire.

SMITH. Come now. She seems to admire you –

GEORGE. No doubt she does.

SMITH. And as an author she is sensational.

GEORGE. Yes… As an author she is indeed admirable. But as a woman she is quite unloveable.

> *(The tinnitus sounds again, but this time prolonged.* **CHARLOTTE** *stands frozen to the spot.)*

> *(Eventually the other characters have enough of the noise and clear off the stage, leaving* **CHARLOTTE** *alone in the emptied out party room.)*

> *(Her breathing quickening in an oncoming panic attack, she bashes aggressively on the door of the ladies loos, trying to hold back tears.)*

ANNE. Just leave me alone, would you Charlotte?

CHARLOTTE. *(Calling through the door.)* Anne?? I need you!!

> *(She bashes on the door again.)*

Anne, I just need to ask you something!!

> *(She bashes at the door again.)*

ANNE??

ANNE. Please… I just don't want to talk to you right now.

> *(***CHARLOTTE*** *backs away from the door, surprised.)*

CHARLOTTE. Why?

Anne?

> *(***ANNE*** *emerges, weary.* **CHARLOTTE** *notices her demeanour,)*

ANNE. Fine. What do you want to ask me?

CHARLOTTE. What's wrong?

(**ANNE** *scoffs an incredulous half laugh –
she's as quietly furious as we've seen her.*)

ANNE. We are in the ladies loos.

CHARLOTTE. What's your point?

ANNE. I am *still* in the ladies loos. I have been here –
hiding here – all night.

CHARLOTTE. You have a dodgy tummy? Was it the eggs?
Tell me it wasn't the eggs. I had two.

(**ANNE** *gives up trying to make a point,
resigned. She sighs.*)

ANNE. What did you want to ask me, Charlotte?

(**CHARLOTTE** *flaps, nervous and
embarrassed.*)

CHARLOTTE. Oh right. Yes. I um... Just something
happened again, with a guy that I ... Well, it's like... I,
ahh, I mean, I'm not like...

(*A small, nervous laugh.*)

... Fundamentally unloveable. Am I?

(**CHARLOTTE** *looks to her little sister,
genuinely imploring.*)

(**ANNE** *sighs, exhausted. Beaten down, she
doesn't make eye contact with* **CHARLOTTE**.)

ANNE. No, Charlotte. You're not unloveable.

CHARLOTTE. OK, so it's just that George Smith was being
a complete –

ANNE. (*Pained but angry.*) You can be hard to love though.

>   (**CHARLOTTE** *looks up at her, stung... She's never heard* **ANNE** *speak like this.*)

Sometimes.

Sometimes you can be *really* hard to love.

>   (**CHARLOTTE** *nervously utters something of a laugh again, wondering if this is some weird joke. She sees it's not. Her face falls.* **ANNE** *stares at the floor.*)

>   (*Not knowing how to process what* **ANNE** *has said,* **CHARLOTTE** *goes on the offensive.*)

CHARLOTTE. Unlike you.

ANNE. We're not talking about me.

CHARLOTTE. What's it like, to be you?

ANNE. Don't lash out –

CHARLOTTE. To look like you do? To be acceptable? To be good?

ANNE. You know I've never felt that way nor cared to.

CHARLOTTE. Well you should care. Because you will never be anything more.

ANNE. Charlotte –

CHARLOTTE. You're still not getting it, are you? You can be in that room Anne, but you will never belong here.

ANNE. Please –

CHARLOTTE. You know your writing is a pale shadow of mine. Of Emily's. You don't *need* to do it.

>   (**ANNE** *is winded by this.*)

ANNE. (*Small, pleading.*) You don't mean that. You don't really mean that.

CHARLOTTE. I'm saying this for your own good. So you can go and *live* life.

Believe me. Go. Marry. Be happy.

I'm just going to say it, if you carry on you'll only ever be known as the third sister. You already are.

> (**ANNE** *nods, gathering herself.*)

ANNE. You see *this* is why.

This is why you are –

CHARLOTTE. Unloveable.

ANNE. Hard to love.

> (*Something has broken between them. It's not 'them' anymore.* **CHARLOTTE** *has ruined the team.*)

I just want to go home, OK? I've done what you asked me. We got what you wanted. I just want to go be with Emily now.

CHARLOTTE. (*Making to apologise.*) Anne –

> (**CHARLOTTE** *watches as* **ANNE** *rushes across the space and throws herself into* **EMILY**'s *arms. How it is the two of them united now.*)

> (*She turns to the audience, imploringly, but is interrupted before she has a chance to speak:*)

BRANWELL. No fun, being the enemy, is it?

> (**CHARLOTTE** *turns –* **BRANWELL** *is beside her. His masculine attire gone, he's in a neutral smock.* **CHARLOTTE** *takes in his change of appearance.*)

CHARLOTTE. Branwell? What's happened to you?

BRANWELL. And you hadn't even noticed.

> (**BRANWELL** *looks to* **EMILY** *and* **ANNE** *by
> way of response.* **EMILY** *disentangles herself
> from her hug with* **ANNE** *and addresses*
> **CHARLOTTE**.*)*

EMILY. It's over.

CHARLOTTE. No –

EMILY. He's dead.

CHARLOTTE. No – no – this is happening too quickly –

> (**BRANWELL** *shrugs at* **CHARLOTTE** *then
> disappears as* **EMILY** *turns and goes to help*
> **ANNE** *bury their brother.)*

(To audience.) No – I was there! I *was* there for them!

> (**EMILY** *and* **ANNE** *pull down on ropes to lower
> the dome of jackets until they all collapse on
> the floor of the stage. The ropes still attached,
> they make the space, their home, into a
> spiders web.)*

But you've *got* to understand. I had already failed as a
woman. I could not now fail as an author. Because it
was *then* that I realised that the most valuable part of
me, *the only loveable part* of me, was in fact owned by
you.

Readers.

So *still*, I *cannot* fail… Or I would lose you all.

> *(She notices* **EMILY** *leaving* **BRANWELL***'s
> funeral.)*

Hey! Hey, perhaps we should all go to Grey's Inn, once
the guests have gone? Raise a glass.

EMILY. *(Dryly.)* Fitting tribute to an alcoholic.

CHARLOTTE. S' what he would have wanted.

EMILY. You know sometimes I wonder if we're even sisters.

> (**CHARLOTTE** *turns, surprised and stung by the change in tone.* **EMILY** *remains pensive.*)

CHARLOTTE. What do you mean?

EMILY. You don't look the same as us, you don't see things the same as us, you don't even think the same as us.

> (,)

CHARLOTTE. Alright...

EMILY. It feels unnatural.

CHARLOTTE. What does?

EMILY. This... Because, despite all those differences you have always been my big sister.

There is something so powerful about that role, isn't there? That dynamic. It's as instinctual as a little girl needing her mother. It's ingrained in us... All these years I have so looked up to you as a big sister.

CHARLOTTE. *(Referring to her height, attempting light.)* That's ironic.

EMILY. Mm... It's why it feels so unnatural to look at you like this now.

CHARLOTTE. Like what?

EMILY. Like you're nothing.

> (,)

Because you might be *my* big sister, but *I* am Anne's... And you should know, if you were but half the little woman you are, that as a big sister your role is to protect and defend your little sister from any harm that comes her way. You should be the person she can go to for safety, *you should* have been the one to be there for her, to lift her up and support her, not steal and bully and suppress her. Not dash all her hopes to feed your own appetite.

CHARLOTTE. No, you've misunderstood. I *am* protecting her.

EMILY. Sure you are. You know you've never dared compete with me like you have her. Because you needed someone lower, someone you found less threatening to step on to reach the heights you so ardently desired. And she has been stupid and kind enough to let you. And I will never, never forgive you for it.

CHARLOTTE. *(Imploring.)* Emily, I ...

> *(**EMILY** waits, expectantly.)*

> *(Small pause.)*

I will not apologise for my success.

> *(**EMILY** raises her eyebrows, surprised.)*

I have not used her. This is – it's, it's what the world would have you think. It's. It's how we're taught to think. We cannot allow a woman success without believing that it has come at another woman's expense, but I – I have done nothing to suppress her. You only think that way because my work has done better. If it had not, then you wouldn't be saying this. I – I really believe that.

> *(**EMILY** smiles, wryly.)*

EMILY. You're good. You really are.

> *(Small pause.)*

> *(**CHARLOTTE** turns to the audience.)*

CHARLOTTE. That was the last we spoke.

The day of Branwell's funeral was the same day Emily started showing signs of having contracted his illness. Refusing help, she wasted away fast.

She was angry right up to the end. With me, with the world, with life for having the audacity to be through with such a kindred spirit as her by thirty. So angry she refused to believe it.

She stood the day she died. She wanted to get out.

>   (**ANNE** *appears. She helps* **EMILY** *out of her dress, down to a neutral smock. Over which:*)

Shining and lowering and swelling and dying,

Changing for ever from midnight to noon;

Roaring like thunder, like soft music sighing,

Shadows on shadows advancing and flying,

Lightning-bright flashes the deep gloom defying,

Coming as swiftly and fading as soon.

>   (**ANNE** *and* **EMILY** *embrace.*)

>   (**EMILY** *starts to leave the stage, but turns over the next:*)

That was hers.

She was always the greatest poet out of all of us. But um...

I did edit that.

Actually. After she died.

EMILY. *(Fuming.)* Are you *JOKING*?!

>   (**CHARLOTTE** *tries not to get derailed by* **EMILY**.)

CHARLOTTE. So I suppose in a way, that's mine too. Now.

EMILY. *(To* **ANNE**.*)* IS SHE *JOKING*?!

CHARLOTTE. In fact, there pretty much wasn't a piece of their work that I didn't edit, after they died.

There were mistakes! And we can't have mistakes.

(She picks up a piece of chalk.)

Although, thinking about it, that rhyme scheme, that language, has gone out of fashion now, so I could just…

EMILY. Oh HELL no… *PUT. THE CHALK. DOWN.*

*(***CHARLOTTE*** catches eyes with her sister, emits a tiny terrified laugh and drops the chalk.)*

*(***EMILY*** backs off, but signs an 'I'm watching you' and remains on stage, keeping an eye on* **CHARLOTTE***'s storytelling.)*

*(***CHARLOTTE*** turns back to the audience, rumbled and trying to get them to understand.)*

Because, there, you see! It's very hard to keep up. It's very very hard to keep up once you're dead. But still one needs to keep revising because of all of you!

'The context'.

You, you *keep* revising and you put us up on a pedestal and yet you *still* find us wanting, but that was the bargain I made when I said I wished to be forever known.

Which makes this hard to tell without, um, mistakes.

*(***CHARLOTTE*** looks about her. The stage is empty.)*

CHARLOTTE. I, um…

(She takes a deep breath, steeling herself. She tries to speak matter of factly.)

So first, she comes to my room and she tells me she's not feeling well.

*(**ANNE** enters. **CHARLOTTE** does not acknowledge her. **EMILY** leans in.)*

ANNE. Charlotte, I'm not feeling well.

CHARLOTTE. I hug her.

EMILY. Liar.

*(**CHARLOTTE** tries to ignore **EMILY**.)*

ANNE. Charlotte?

*(**CHARLOTTE** ignores **ANNE**.)*

CHARLOTTE. Then one day she falls. In the kitchen.

*(**ANNE** falls. **CHARLOTTE** remains where she is over the following:)*

I go to her and I hold her and I know then that she's dying.

ANNE. I'm scared.

CHARLOTTE. Of course, I do whatever I can to help her.

EMILY. Liar – tell the truth.

CHARLOTTE. We get the doctor Emily refused to see.

ANNE. I'm sorry –

CHARLOTTE. She was her good, sweet, quiet self all the while.

ANNE. I can't stay here. I –

*(**CHARLOTTE** turns to **ANNE**, interrupting.)*

CHARLOTTE. Enough!

Can you not *just* –! I am *trying* to work.

(*She glances about the audience, embarrassed, like a bad host.*)

Can you not see?

ANNE. Sorry. Sorry. I just... I'm going to Scarborough. For the sea air.

(**CHARLOTTE** *glances to* **EMILY** *who nods in encouragement from the sidelines.* **CHARLOTTE** *turns into the scene, facing* **ANNE.**)

CHARLOTTE. You can't go, you won't make the journey.

ANNE. I think it's my only chance. They say the water is healing.

CHARLOTTE. No. It will do you more harm than good.

ANNE. Please. I really don't want to... Not like Emily.

CHARLOTTE. You're not sick like Emily.

(**ANNE** *nods.*)

ANNE. OK.

CHARLOTTE. Honestly. You're not.

ANNE. OK.

CHARLOTTE. You believe me?

ANNE. (*Small.*) Yes.

Only... Do you think we can go anyway? Or I can go by myself? I just – I want to see the sea.

CHARLOTTE. Fine.

(*She turns back to the audience.*)

So we go to Scarborough. And she looked at the sea and I looked at her and neither of us could really fathom what we were looking at.

(Her distress finally gets the better of her.)

My sister.

(She tries to shake it off and get back to the story.)

She held my hand. So peaceful. An angel.

*(**EMILY** takes **ANNE** away from **CHARLOTTE**.)*

And I take her back to the rooms we had rented.

*(With **EMILY**'s help **ANNE** slowly begins to pick off the layers of female dress, down into her neutral smock over the next.)*

*(Whilst **CHARLOTTE** speaks, she busily rearranges the stage to create the perfect scene. She raises the male jackets up from the floor and sends them flying out of view. She fills the space above them with a blanket of stars. She fixes the lighting to a warm colour, fills the space with sounds of the sea. etc.)*

And lay her in the little bed.

And then I rearrange the stars to make space for her arrival and everything and everyone is silent. Only a silence that still could come close to that final, perfect, untroubled sleep.

*(**ANNE** disappears with **EMILY** to the edges of the space.)*

(Pause.)

*(**CHARLOTTE** looks about the empty scene she has created and scoffs at it, unimpressed.)*

(She returns to the audience with anger.)

You know for centuries male authors, my idols, have written us perfect deaths. Glorious deaths. Deaths in which we look more beautiful than we did in life. Deaths in which we become pure. Deaths so apparently holy and apparently innocent they have made headlines and shaken governments and moved whole armies into battle and now I know why.

*(**CHARLOTTE** starts to write over the floor, her third novel,* Shirley.*)*

*(**ANNE** voices the character Caroline from the novel, lying on her 'deathbed' with **EMILY** comforting her.)*

ANNE. "You are weeping at the pathos of the air. Come here, and I will comfort you".

CHARLOTTE. "Said Caroline, in a pitying accent. Mrs Pryor came. She sat down on the edge of her patient's bed and allowed the wasted arms to encircle her".

*(**EMILY** begins to corpse.)*

ANNE. "You often soothe me, let me soothe you".

CHARLOTTE. "Murmured the young girl, kissing her cheek".

*(**ANNE** does so to **EMILY**, who is now clearly struggling not to burst out laughing. It's infectious and **ANNE** begins to corpse also.)*

ANNE. "I hope".

CHARLOTTE. "She added".

ANNE. *(Laughing.)* "It is not for me that you weep?"

*(**CHARLOTTE** slams her chalk down. **EMILY** bursts into a cackle.)*

CHARLOTTE. What's so funny?!

EMILY. Sorry. Sorry.

CHARLOTTE. What are you doing?

EMILY. Sorry – it's just so shit. This scene is so shit.

ANNE. Emily!

CHARLOTTE. Excuse me?

(To audience.) My third novel – *Shirley* – sure you've heard of it. It's *great*.

EMILY. Never mind.

CHARLOTTE. *(Pointed.)* No, go on. If you've got a 'note' …

EMILY. You *know* the 'note'.

CHARLOTTE. No I don't know the 'note'.

EMILY. Tell her Anne.

ANNE. No, let her write the thing –

EMILY. Go on, tell her –

CHARLOTTE. Go on, tell me.

ANNE. Well, I – I – I was never like this! She's based on me right? Caroline?

CHARLOTTE. Yes. I wanted to give you a happy ending.

EMILY. You were gonna kill her off a minute ago.

CHARLOTTE. Sure but then she went and actually died and I missed her. *(To **ANNE**.)* I *missed* you!

ANNE. But I was never like this! I was never meek! In *Shirley*, in your head, *(Gesturing to the stage/audience.)* in whatever this is… *(To **CHARLOTTE**.)* I was never a mouse. I – I – I never had this weird stutter you've given me, I was never actually this blonde and my death *fully sucked.*

CHARLOTTE. I'm protecting you! I'm making you the likeable one.

EMILY. Bullshit. You're competing still.

ANNE. *(To **EMILY**.)* No, I for one believe her. I think it's both. We're sisters!

You can miss me and want to protect me and also be so jealous of me you want to destroy me –

CHARLOTTE. Christ no! I didn't. I never. I –

> *(She is interrupted as their maid **TABBY** enters. The scene disappearing as she does so.)*

TABBY. Miss Brontë?

> *(**CHARLOTTE** turns to her. Dazed.)*

CHARLOTTE. What?

TABBY. Sorry –

CHARLOTTE. I'm working.

TABBY. Sorry. It's just there's people at the door.

CHARLOTTE. What people?

TABBY. I do not know ma'am.

CHARLOTTE. Did you not ask them who they were?

TABBY. Yes ma'am, I mean I do not know them. They are readers of your work.

CHARLOTTE. What? How? How does this *keep* happening?

TABBY. I'm sorry, I –

CHARLOTTE. Send them away. Say only Miss Brontë lives here. Say they have made a mistake.

> (**CHARLOTTE** *turns to the audience.* **TABBY**
> *disappearing as she does so.*)

Rumours had spread. I'd given too much away, people
had seen me and I couldn't resist writing back to the
few famous authors who had found me out because...
That was what I had always wanted! Wasn't it? To
engage with minds like that as equals. Because that was
the aim. Because... Well, who else was there to talk to?!

> (**GEORGE** *enters,* **VICTORIAN READERS** *and*
> **CRITICS** *behind him, carrying long panes of*
> *glass. He extends an arm.*)

GEORGE. Miss Brontë?

> (*Reluctantly* **CHARLOTTE** *goes to meet him.*
> *He guides her to the centre of the stage, onto a*
> *small podium.*)

> (*Music starts to play as she goes. Donna*
> *Summer's "I Feel Love".*)

> (*The* **READERS** *encase* **CHARLOTTE** *in a glass*
> *box. She starts to dance for them, with them,*
> *as they do so. It's a party, a celebration of*
> **CHARLOTTE**.)

CHARLOTTE. I was an idol!

A female fucking idol!

Finally!

(*A lie.*) And I wasn't lonely *AT ALL!*

> (**CHARLOTTE** *dances the track through from*
> *within her glass case. Her movements are*
> *wild, sexual, modern.*)

> (*Around her the* **READERS**, **CRITICS**, *and*
> **GEORGE** *dance also in frenzied, sped up*

traditional moves. Like a period drama dance scene on coke.)

*(Throughout individuals break their dancing to gape at **CHARLOTTE**; mocking, entertained, in awe... These make her flinch, but she keeps dancing for them.)*

*(**GEORGE SMITH** cuts the music and raises a glass to the room.)*

GEORGE. Ladies and gentlemen, I give you the author you have previously known and loved as Mr Currer Bell, the voice of a generation, Miss Charlotte Brontë!!

*(**GEORGE** turns to **CHARLOTTE** in her glass case, gesturing for her to address everyone and **CHARLOTTE** begins what looks like a wide smiled acceptance speech... Only we can't hear her from behind the glass.)*

THACKERAY. Bit of a let down. If I'm honest.

*(**CHARLOTTE** looks perturbed. The rest of her onlookers don't seem to give a damn they can't hear her. They prowl the space around her, curiously taking in her image, like she's a piece of art on display.)*

HARRIET MARTINEAU. She is the smallest creature I have seen, except at a fair.

*(Worried at this, **CHARLOTTE** plasters on her best smile. She poses, mutely for them in what she hopes is an appropriately demure and feminine attitude.)*

CRITIC 1. So innocent and un-Londony!

CRITIC 2. She seems so anxious!

(From within her case, CHARLOTTE mouths a 'Well, Duh'. Because anyone would be anxious in her position right now. She's ignored. She anxiously gets back to trying to look appropriately pretty and retiring.)

LEWES. It's a little bit, erm... Titillating.

THACKERAY. Titillating?

FONBLANQUE. I get that.

MARTINEAU. Actually, I find her intolerably painful.

(All turn to MARTINEAU. Also struck by her words, CHARLOTTE stops posing to listen.)

Not only does an atmosphere of pain hang over her work, but all her female characters, in all their thoughts and lives are full of nothing but love.

CRITIC 1. Yes, her heroines love too readily, too vehemently –

CRITIC 2. *(Agreeing.)* And after a fashion her female readers might resent...

CRITIC 1. So coarse. So ugly.

MARTINEU. It makes us wonder about her life... If in life she loves more than she is beloved.

(CHARLOTTE freezes, winded by this last, resting a hand against the glass to steady herself. She looks to ANNE and EMILY longingly.)

(The CRITICS disappear.)

(ANNE tries to make towards CHARLOTTE to help, but EMILY holds her back.)

(GEORGE appears, with work.)

GEORGE. Admin!

CHARLOTTE. Sure. What have we got?

GEORGE. Just wondered if you wanted to reply to these.

CHARLOTTE. *(To* **ANNE.**) I can feel you looking at me –

> (**GEORGE** *looks up from his papers.)*

GEORGE. What?

CHARLOTTE. Nothing.

Um. Yes. Yes, leave them there.

GEORGE. Great.

> (**CHARLOTTE** *glances towards* **ANNE**
> *nervously.* **GEORGE** *follows her eye-line*
> *warily, himself seeing nothing.)*

And then just a few thoughts on *Shirley...* Nothing
major. Few inconsistencies –

CHARLOTTE. Like what?

GEORGE. Well –

> *(He makes to sit down where* **ANNE** *is.*
> **CHARLOTTE** *raps the glass –)*

CHARLOTTE. Not there!

> (**GEORGE** *stands up straight, emitting a*
> *small hollow laugh at her behaviour.)*

GEORGE. "The tables' full"?

CHARLOTTE. What?

GEORGE. Um. *Macbeth.*

CHARLOTTE. Did you just tell me that was from *Macbeth*?

GEORGE. Um. Yes.

CHARLOTTE. You didn't think *I* would know that was from *Macbeth*?

GEORGE. I, um...

CHARLOTTE. You, um...

GEORGE. No –

CHARLOTTE. No –

GEORGE. No, course you knew it was from *Macbeth*.

CHARLOTTE. What are the inconsistencies George?

GEORGE. Well there's, just things like... In – in lots of the scenes you say the character Caroline has brown eyes, but then in this one scene you say she has, um, blue eyes.

> (**CHARLOTTE** *regards him flatly from her glass case.*)

I'll just leave them here.

CHARLOTTE. Good.

I, ah...

> (**CHARLOTTE** *openly wrestles with herself. She grows increasingly uncomfortable and agitated:*)

GEORGE. Are you sure you're alright?

CHARLOTTE. *(Forced, pained.)* Yes. I just.. I need to ask you, because this is what I asked you...

(Light.) Is there anything else?

GEORGE. Yes, actually, um... Your sister's novel. *The Tenant of Wildfell Hall* has sold out again.

CHARLOTTE. It has?

GEORGE. Good news.

CHARLOTTE. Yeah. Great...

GEORGE. So just checking I've got your permission to reprint it? You have all the rights to your sisters' work, so I just need clearance.

(**ANNE** *leans in.* **CHARLOTTE** *notices.*)

CHARLOTTE. Why?

GEORGE. Why?

CHARLOTTE. Yes, why? If all the copies are gone then all the copies are gone.

GEORGE. Are you alright?

CHARLOTTE. Yes, I just don't see why it needs to be reprinted.

GEORGE. Because... Well because, if anything we think it's only going to gain in popularity. It becomes more relevant every day. You want her legacy to live on, don't you?

CHARLOTTE. Mm.

(,)

GEORGE. So? Do I have your permission?

(**CHARLOTTE** *looks up at him.*)

CHARLOTTE. No.

GEORGE. No?

(**GEORGE** *pauses, stunned.*)

CHARLOTTE. It was a mistake.

GEORGE. A mistake?

CHARLOTTE. My sister, Mr Smith, was an angel.

GEORGE. Oh absolutely.

CHARLOTTE. But in writing this she was misguided. Immature... She was *trying* to shock — me I think. Trying to prove herself to her big sister. You see? No. I will not have the whole country poking and deriding her. She was a perfect woman. And she shall remain as such. A greater readership would destroy her reputation, not make it.

GEORGE. Really?

CHARLOTTE. You know that.

GEORGE. Well, ah... Without wishing to seem *indelicate* Miss Brontë... Her reputation... In terms of marriage, in terms of, um, 'respectability', is, um, well. Might be *seen* to be, um, beside the point... Now that she's, um, dead.

(,)

CHARLOTTE. Well then... It would destroy mine.

GEORGE. You don't think she is a threat to you? –

CHARLOTTE. And we can't have that.

(,)

GEORGE. You're quite sure?

(*She looks at him from within her case, in pointed accusation.*)

CHARLOTTE. I don't make the rules.

GEORGE. Right, but –

CHARLOTTE. Is that everything?

GEORGE. Um, yes.

CHARLOTTE. Then yes.

Kill it.

> (**GEORGE** *exits, leaving the piles of letters and notes on the outside of* **CHARLOTTE***'s glass case.*)

> (*Pause.*)

> (**CHARLOTTE** *looks to* **ANNE**.)

There.

> (**ANNE** *gestures to* **CHARLOTTE** *to turn around. Sprightly, prim* **ELIZABETH GASKELL** *has appeared.* **GASKELL**, *who* **CHARLOTTE** *is clearly not enamoured with. She taps on the glass.*)

Oh Christ.

GASKELL. Helleeewww!!!

CHARLOTTE. (*To audience.*) Elizabeth Gaskell.

GASKELL. (*Loudly.*) You OK in there??

CHARLOTTE. I'm fiiiine Elizabeth.

(*To audience, deeply fed up.*) Gaskell was my first biographer... At the time she was my friend and sort of colleague. You've probably seen her work on the BBC. There's a lot of bonnets and cake.

GASKELL. I've brought crumpets!

CHARLOTTE. Gaskell was essentially a kiss arse who never really fully got my work, but was sort of well into the 'women supporting women' thing. Her biography of me was actually one of the first ever biographies of a woman, period. *And* it was written by another woman –

> (*She mimes her head exploding.*)

With it she actually sort of formed the whole concept of the modern celebrity biography genre. Which, I guess, *was* cool.

GASKELL. *(To audience.)* I just wanted her to be understood, you know? As a *human* –

CHARLOTTE. No, no – you don't get to speak to them.

GASKELL. Oh. Sorry.

Anyway... I just have some more questions.

CHARLOTTE. *(Weary.)* Why?

GASKELL. Well, if we are to try and make sure you keep up the sort of readership that will place you in the canon, we just need to make all of those controversial opinions in your work a little less... Well, controversial.

(**CHARLOTTE** *smiles wryly.*)

CHARLOTTE. No, I get it.

GASKELL. Girls are still not allowed to read *Jane Eyre*. But if we make *you* acceptable – so holy, so sweet, *such* a *victim*, then we might keep it alive.

(**CHARLOTTE** *closes her eyes, pained.*)

Believe me I'm with you. I want another woman in the ranks. But there is a game that must be played.

CHARLOTTE. But this isn't about me. Is it?

GASKELL. Beg pardon?

CHARLOTTE. It's about you selling this book about me. Which is a lie about me.

GASKELL. Now –

CHARLOTTE. You know I found the other day that my most vicious critique of *Jane Eyre* was written by a woman? Posing as a man, because that was the only way to get her own work into print. She was a man attacking my lack of female propriety, on the suspicion that I, *Currer Bell,* was actually a woman.

That's the game that's being played.

(**GASKELL** *smiles politely. She changes tact...*)

GASKELL. And what about your sisters. They both had dogs. Do you have a dog?

CHARLOTTE. No. I'm more of a cat person.

GASKELL. Me too.

CHARLOTTE. Sure you are.

GASKELL. And growing up without a mother, without a role model, must have been hard for all of you.

CHARLOTTE. No.

No, it wasn't. We made up our own rules. We played together. We worked together.

(*This is upsetting to her.*)

We were happy, you know?

You know we were actually very happy.

(*Small pause.*)

GASKELL. You know I really am only doing this to protect you, right? To protect your work.

(**CHARLOTTE** *wrestles with this, until she is resigned.*)

CHARLOTTE. Yeah, yeah. I get it.

So, so my sisters and I will be memorialised as three sad little women living in the arse end of nowhere, stalked by tragedy and that vague witchy thing people have about women in groups of three so that none of what we thought or wrote that broke through, that broke the mould of what was or wasn't allowed was our *fault*.

Because otherwise it *is* our fault.

In fiction or reality.

Antigone. Joan. Cleopatra. Anna. Desdemona.

Our whole narrative depends on tragedy to forgive our strength.

GASKELL. Or... We've just got to *hope* at some point in the future people will see past all that.

People will see past this version of you that I'm writing. I promise.

> (**CHARLOTTE** *looks back at her.*)

We leave it in the hands of those to come. We tell the lie so that your *work* might be given permission to speak the truth.

CHARLOTTE. And you really believe this?

GASKELL. I do.

> (**CHARLOTTE** *looks to* **ANNE**, *who shrugs in agreement. This panics* **CHARLOTTE**.)

I mean, with Emily it might be a little more of a hard sell –

CHARLOTTE. I'm not concerned about *Wuthering Heights* living on. What about Anne?

GASKELL. Ah, well, to be honest Anne doesn't really feature much. After she died her work sort of faded away with her...

> (**CHARLOTTE** *nods, crestfallen.*)

Don't be hard on yourself. If it wasn't for you it wouldn't get half the readership it does today.

But her reputation is well protected for it. She really is the good one. The sweet one. The quiet, pious one.

Not an *author*, really. Just a woman.

> (**CHARLOTTE** *smiles. A hollow smile.*)

CHARLOTTE. Yes.

GASKELL. But her death will help your story here.

CHARLOTTE. It's not my story. It's not about me.

GASKELL. Oh, but it is... And you know it.

>(**GASKELL** *disappears.*)

>(**CHARLOTTE** *doesn't look at* **ANNE**. *She slides down the glass and sits, a shell.*)

>(**EMILY** *nods for* **ANNE** *to go. She approaches the glass. Puts a hand to it.* **CHARLOTTE** *looks up.*)

ANNE. It's OK.

CHARLOTTE. How?

ANNE. Look... Our time is over. We're nothing, Charlotte.

CHARLOTTE. I destroyed you.

>(**ANNE** *smiles, comfortingly – still a mother to a distressed child.*)

ANNE. So I was never meant to do anything but die. And you were never meant to do anything but live. On and on and on.

People take you and they change you and they make you into something even I don't know.

My poor Charlotte.

You have become everything to so many people.

But, despite whatever you may think, I know that I saw you. And you saw me. And we were each just doing our best at the time. And that is all any of us can ever hope to do.

We're all just doing our best!

At the time.

And it is *good* that that was never enough.

CHARLOTTE. Really?

ANNE. Really. Let them judge...

> *(She glances back at* **EMILY***, waiting for them.)*

Come and be with us now.

CHARLOTTE. I want to... But I'm scared.

ANNE. You can do it.

> *(***CHARLOTTE** *nods, preparing herself.)*

You've got to let them take over.

Because we know that there will always be more to do. To correct. We must constantly reexamine in order to move forward.

> *(***ANNE** *looks about the space – the abandoned props, the chalk covered floor – the ruins of* **CHARLOTTE***'s imagination...)*

To breath life into something that is, really, nothing.

Because, dear sister, here we are, yet again.

Everything to each other.

And yet... Nothing.

> *(Black.)*

End

Milton Keynes UK
Ingram Content Group UK Ltd.
UKHW021835050624
443484UK00007B/50